God's Family
What the Bible Says about the Church

Churches Alive
Box 3800
San Bernardino, CA 92413
Phone (714) 886-5361

3/83

SPECIAL THANKS to the following staff members of Churches Alive for their contributions in developing the *God's Family* study:

Media staff — for the writing, creative concepts, editing, layout and production: Ronald A. Wormser, Media Director; Russ Korth, Curriculum Editor (who also researched and prepared the original manuscript); Ron Wormser Jr., Media Editor; Juanita Arroues, Media Coordinator; Cecile Watkins, Media Secretary; and Frank Dolan, Print Coordinator.

Other Churches Alive staff — for their study, evaluation and interaction: Howard Ball, President; Ron Jones, Field Director; Henry Schneider, Special Representative; and Gordon Shipps, Business Manager.

Copyright © Churches Alive, 1983.

Library of Congress No. 82-72563
ISBN: *God's Family* 0-934396-34-5
　　　God's Family Leader's Guide Edition 0-934396-35-3

All rights reserved. No part of this publication may be reproduced, stored in a retrieval system or transmitted in any form or by any means, electronic, mechanical, photocopy, recording or otherwise, without the written permission of the copyright owner.

Churches Alive is a non-profit organization. Gifts for the purpose of helping this ministry serve the local church are tax-deductible.

Except where noted, Scripture quotations are from the New American Standard Bible, ©The Lockman Foundation 1960, 1962, 1963, 1968, 1971, 1972, 1973, 1975.

First Printing, March 1983.

Printed in the United States of America.

Photography by Per Volquartz.

Contents

	GOD'S FAMILY	5
Chapter 1	YOU'RE IN THE FAMILY	7
Chapter 2	FAMILY BOND	15
Chapter 3	FAMILY POWER	23
Chapter 4	FAMILY RELATIONS	31
Chapter 5	FAMILY NEEDS	41
Chapter 6	FAMILY WORSHIP	49
Chapter 7	FAMILY HOUSE	57
Chapter 8	FAMILY CONFLICT	63
Chapter 9	FAMILY GOAL	71
Chapter 10	FAMILY TEAM	79
Chapter 11	FAMILY LEADERS	87
Chapter 12	FAMILY COMMITMENT	95
	DISCIPLING HELPS	103

NOTE:
A special leader's guide section begins on page 113 of the *Leader's Guide Edition* of *God's Family*.

God's Family

ERNIE WAS A BALD EAGLE with full plumage, a sharp beak and strong talons. He embodied all the aspects of the proud tradition of eagles — all but one. Ernie couldn't fly.

When he was still an eaglet, he heard he would be pushed out of the nest.

"That's how you'll learn to fly."

"I don't want to be pushed out of the nest," he replied.

"But then you'll never soar."

"I don't want to be pushed out!"

"But eagles need to fly to gather food."

"I don't want to be pushed."

"But..."

Ernie heard right. He would have been pushed out of the nest to learn to fly. But he never would have fallen to the ground. His mother would have lifted him back to the nest repeatedly until he mastered flying skills.

Today many Christians, like Ernie, have fixed their minds on a half-truth that prevents them from enjoying the benefits of full participation in God's family — the Church. As you complete the exercises in this book, you will learn about God's family as He designed it so you can experience fulfillment in the Church.

"...those who wait for the Lord... will mount up with wings like eagles..." (Isaiah 40:31)

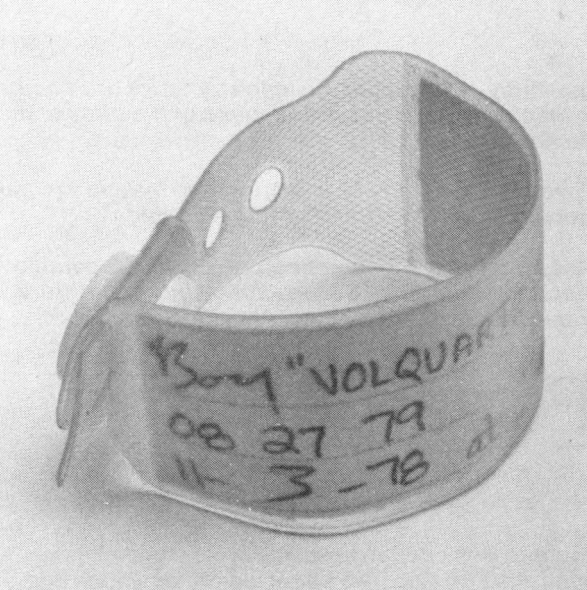

You're in the Family

CHAPTER 1

Repeatedly, throughout His ministry, our Lord used simple illustrations to teach profound truths. He spoke of the birds of the air and the lilies of the field.

He used the parable — "A short narrative making a moral or religious point by comparison with natural or homely things."

In this study, each chapter begins with such a parable — pointedly simple. But the thought questions following each story will lead to penetrating insights regarding God's family — the Church.

A Parable

THE FIRST WORKMAN WHO SAW Curved Brick laughed out loud and threw him aside. "This one is useless."

Curved Brick began to have doubts about himself. "Maybe I'm not a brick at all. I could be a paper weight or a book end." But deep inside, he knew he should be part of the building.

Some of the other bricks were discussing whether Curved Brick could ever fit in with them, when Architect visited the building site. The workmen had asked him to come and explain part of the blueprints so they could complete the building. When Architect saw their dilemma, he asked for Curved Brick. Sheepishly, one worker pointed to the trash heap. No one offered any excuse when they saw the scowl on Architect's face.

Curved Brick couldn't believe it! Architect, himself, came to the pile to pull him from the debris, dust him off and set him in place in the building. "I personally *designed* this brick to fit here."

Curved Brick felt so good to be where he belonged.

NOTE:
Use the "Think about It" sections for personal meditation and to prepare for group discussion. It is not necessary to record your answers.

Think about It

What is the main point of the story?

How has God designed you to fit into His building?

Have you ever felt you were on the trash heap like Curved Brick?

When?

Why do you think the builder didn't use Curved Brick at first?

What does this illustrate in life?

God's Child

"For now we are all children of God through faith in Jesus Christ." (Galatians 3:26 — Living Bible) You are part of His family. It may be difficult to imagine God as a proud father showing your picture to others and telling them how much He thinks of you. But God is that kind of a father.

ONE. The longer you meditate on the fact that you are a member of God's family, the more amazed you will become at the position you have. Give one reason you consider it a privilege to be in God's family.

TWO. Read 1 John 3:1-3. What motivated God to make you His child?

As God's child, to what can you look forward?

How will this "hope" affect you now?

THREE. According to Romans 8:16,17, what is included in being a child of God?

Born into the Family

When you were born, you became a member of an earthly family. In the same way, you entered into the great privilege of being part of God's family by spiritual birth. This occurs after your first birth. It's called the "second birth," the "rebirth" and "regeneration."

FOUR. Read John 1:11-13 and John 3:3-7 and give three important facts about your new birth. (More than three are given.)

1.

2.

3.

Father of the Family

Being part of God's family is more than a position, more than a title and more than a series of benefits. It is a relationship with God, Himself. He is actively involved in your life as a father.

FIVE. What does God do for you?

Psalm 103:12-14

Matthew 7:7-11

Romans 8:14,15

SIX. In one of the best known of His parables, Jesus taught about God's actions as a father. Read the story of the prodigal son in Luke 15:11-32 and answer the following questions.

What are some things this story illustrates about the father?

(Question 6 continued on next page)

12 — God's Family   You're in the Family

What lesson can be learned from the actions of the younger son?

What lesson can be learned from the actions of the older son?

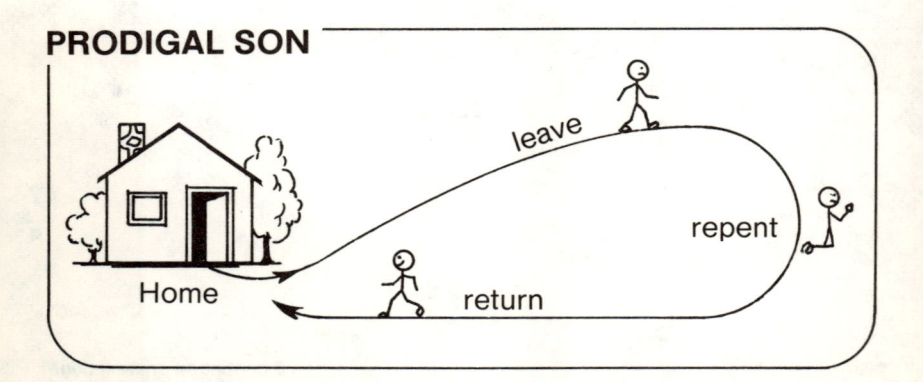

PRODIGAL SON

A Prayerful Response

Father, thank You for being my father, for giving me life and spiritual breath through my Lord Jesus Christ. I am amazed that You think so much of me that You take care of me personally — that You lead me, guide me, listen to me. Thank You for sending Your Holy Spirit to live inside me.

I recognize that I am prone to wander away from You. Thank You for always taking me back in love and forgiveness. Thank You that I have a church family of brothers and sisters who love me and care for me. I love them, too. But most of all, I love You. AMEN.

Family Bond

CHAPTER 2

A Parable

LILA LEAF GREW on an upper branch of a tall oak. She shared a twig with brothers and sisters and Mom and Dad. Cousins filled adjoining branches, while farther away distant relatives resided.

Almost daily, cavorting winds tempted Lila to let go and enjoy a soaring and swirling ride. Later, in the stillness and sunshine, the aroma of the flowers below would drift through the tree branches. Lila longed to flutter down to appreciate the fragrance in all its potency.

One day, Lila was telling her sister how difficult she found it, at times, to remain in the tree. "Why don't you leave?" asked a spider spinning a web in nearby branches.

"Oh, it sounds like such fun," Lila replied. "But if I leave the family tree, I'll die."

Think about It

In what sense do we die if we are cut off from the "tree" of our fellowship?

What are other ways we, as Christians, are like plants or parts of plants?

What are some things Lila Leaf does for the leaves that are on the far side of the tree? How is this similar to things that happen in God's family?

Love Is the Bond

The sharing of love bonds the members of God's family. They show care and concern because they enjoy it. Love in the family is modeled after the freely given love of God. "In this is love, not that we loved God, but that He loved us and sent His Son to be the propitiation* for our sins. Beloved, if God so loved us, we also ought to love one another." (1 John 4:10,11)

---

*propitiation: the sacrificial payment

Family Bond   *God's Family — 17*

ONE. Complete the chain from 1 John 5:1,2.

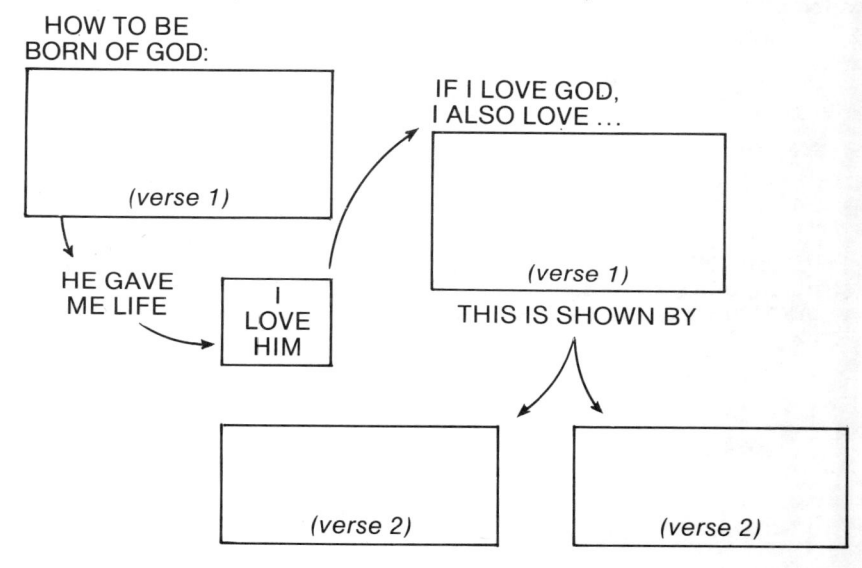

HOW TO BE
BORN OF GOD:

[(verse 1)]

IF I LOVE GOD,
I ALSO LOVE ...

[(verse 1)]

HE GAVE ME LIFE → [I LOVE HIM]

THIS IS SHOWN BY

[(verse 2)] [(verse 2)]

TWO. Loving God includes loving the other members of His family. This means you can enjoy the benefits of being enveloped by the love of others while at the same time carrying out your responsibility to love them, too.

Several examples of overflowing love can be seen in Paul's letter to his friend, Philemon. What is one way love was demonstrated in each verse below?

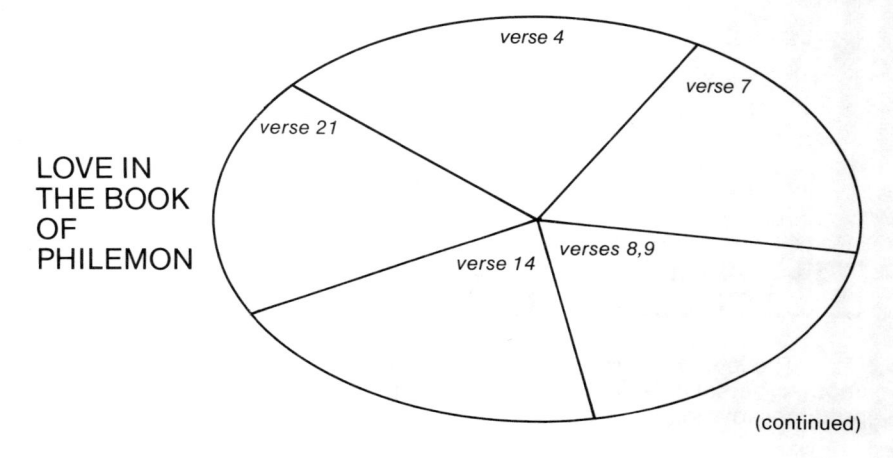

LOVE IN THE BOOK OF PHILEMON

- verse 4
- verse 7
- verse 21
- verse 14
- verses 8,9

(continued)

Which of the demonstrations of love you listed on the previous page do you appreciate the most? Why?

THREE. One love responsibility you have is to "consider how to stimulate one another to love and good deeds." *(Hebrews 10:24)* What is one of the most effective ways others can stimulate you to love?

What are some ways your church family fosters love among each other?

The Nature of Love

The love the Scriptures talk about begins with an attitude of wanting another person's benefit regardless of the cost. This loving *attitude* produces loving *actions*.

Family Bond **God's Family — 19**

FOUR. 1 Corinthians 13 describes actions that reflect love. Using verses 4-7 for reference, write a short paragraph (or a poem) about one of the subjects below.

Love is patient

Love is kind

Love is unselfish

Love is honest

FIVE. Read Galatians 5:13-23 and list at least three things associated with love and three things associated with a lack of love.

LOVE	LACK OF LOVE

SIX. An action may show love in one situation and not in another. For example, a handshake may communicate love, or it may seem cool and indifferent. What keeps actions from being hollow expressions of love?

Effects of Love

LOVE —Produces→ ACTION —Affects→ WORLD

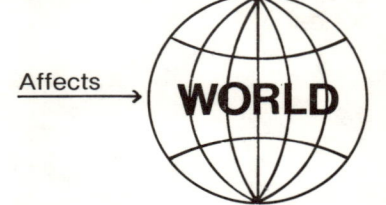

> When Gloria was returned to her hospital room after surgery, she had a new roommate. Susan, a former motorcycle gang member, had a body that was marred by bullet holes and drugs; but her needs went far deeper than that. She was hungry for love and deeply impressed by the love demonstrated by Gloria's visitors. Friends from her church came daily. The holding of hands in prayer, the conversations, the hugs — all ministered in a way that few sermons could. Susan's heart was so opened to God that later, when she and Gloria watched a church service on television, Susan said every word of the message was meant especially for her.

SEVEN. Susan was touched by the fact that Gloria was enveloped by love from other people in God's family. How are you affected when you see a group bound together by love?

Family Bond

How does it affect you when you are part of a group bound together by love?

EIGHT. What effect did Jesus say love would have? *John 13:34,35*

A Prayerful Response

I love You, God; and I know You love me, too. When I think of Your love for me, I feel very close to You. I don't think I can comprehend Your love in sending Your Son, Jesus Christ, to die for me.

Thank You for making me part of Your Body, Your Family, Your Church. I am not alone — there are so many that love me. I love them, too. Each week as we get together, I see new ways to show love.

I praise You for the Holy Spirit inside me Who produces unselfish acts. (I know how self-centered I am without Him.) There is love to me, for me, around me and in me. May I reflect it to others. AMEN.

Family Power

CHAPTER 3

A Parable

AT FIRST HE THOUGHT he didn't try hard enough. So with renewed vigor and determination, he set out to light up the house. And he failed again.

Little Lamp felt discouraged. He wanted desperately to give light.

He heard about a "light" seminar, and he attended. One speaker explained the function of light and its importance. Another talked about the glory of light and the doom of darkness. The seminar ended with a dedication ceremony, and the leader struck a match and touched the flame to Little Lamp's wick. When it lit, he was ecstatic.

By the next morning his flame had gone out. All he had was a severely charred wick.

More depressed than ever, he happened to meet Bright Lantern. Lantern listened to Lamp and then, with a knowing smile, told him, "You've misunderstood Lampmaker's plan. *You* don't give light; the flame does. And *you* aren't supposed to burn; oil inside you is. You are only a container for the oil. Go get filled with oil, and see how easy it is for you to give light."

Think about It

What does the story illustrate?

How are we like Little Lamp?

What would be a parallel in your experience to Little Lamp trying harder? to being filled with oil?

What could cause you to run out of oil?

God's Presence

Undoubtedly, the most precious treasure we in God's family enjoy is God, Himself. When you accepted Jesus Christ as your Lord and Savior, God actually took residence in you. Other religions claim that God can

Family Power   *God's Family — 25*

be "for you" or "near you" or "with you." But the Bible declares that when you become a member of God's family through Jesus Christ, you have God living *in you.*

    Jesus said that "... He (the Spirit) abides with you, and will be in you;" *(John 14:17)* "... I am in My Father, and you in Me, and I in you;" *(John 14:20)* "... My Father will love him, and We will ... make Our abode with him." *(John 14:23)*

    ONE. What did Paul call "Christ in you"? *Colossians 1:27*

What does this expression mean to you?

    God living in you is more than a wondrous thing. He has residence in you so He can guide, direct and control your life. He was at work in you to bring you to Himself, and He will continue to work in you.

    TWO. What are some things God's work in you produces? *Philippians 2:13*

God's Power

    THREE. Read Galatians 5:16-23. These verses indicate that a Christian is either walking in the Spirit or walking in the flesh. No other alternative is presented. Use your own words or a modern Bible translation to give another expression for:

WALKING
IN THE
SPIRIT

(continued)

WALKING IN THE FLESH

Read Galatians 5:19-21 and then use your own words to describe the way a person who is walking in the flesh would relate to others.

Read Galatians 5:22 and 23 and then use your own words to describe the way a person who is walking in the Spirit (living by the Spirit) would relate to others.

FOUR. Most people, whether they are Christians or not, would like to be the kind of person you've described as walking in the Spirit. Unfortunately, they find they are unable to fulfill this desire. Why can you consider this weakness an asset? *2 Corinthians 12:9*

Family Power   **God's Family — 27**

FIVE. One of the greatest demonstrations of God's power was the resurrection of Jesus Christ. Jesus was dead — physically, completely dead. But He came to life again. It was not just His Spirit, but bodily and in every way He came to life. Because God is in you, the power that changes death to life is available to you. Romans 6:6-14 describes God's resurrection power at work. Use this passage to complete the diagram below with facts about each subject mentioned in the boxes.

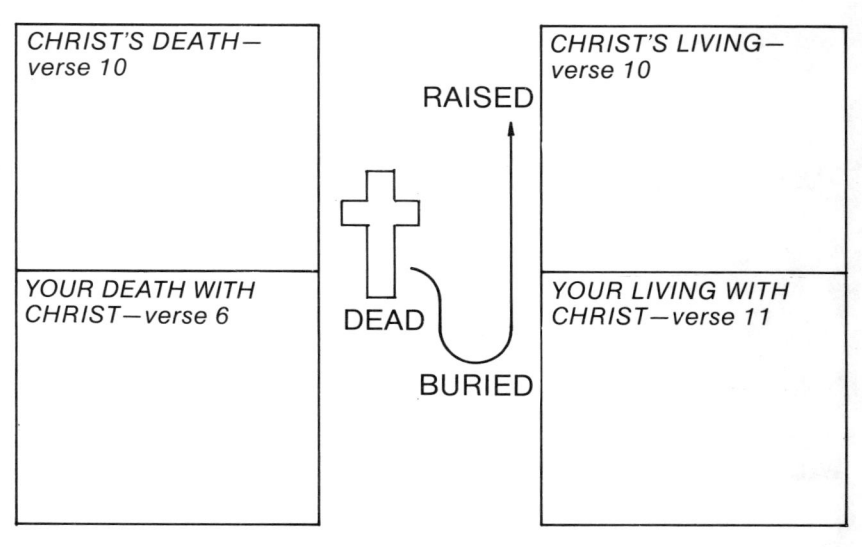

CHRIST'S DEATH— *verse 10*	CHRIST'S LIVING— *verse 10*
YOUR DEATH WITH CHRIST—*verse 6*	YOUR LIVING WITH CHRIST—*verse 11*

RAISED

DEAD

BURIED

On the basis of these truths, you . . .

. . . should not — *verse 13*

. . . should — *verse 13*

SIX. Many concepts about "family power" are summarized in Romans 8:9-14. What is one important teaching about each of the following topics?

God in you. *Verses 9, 10, 11*

God's resurrection power at work in you. *Verse 11*

Walking in (living after) the flesh. *Verses 12, 13*

Walking in (living after) the Spirit. *Verses 13, 14*

A Prayerful Response

It is not reasonable to me that You, the God of Glory, should live in me. You deserve a better throne. You have given me an honor that is beyond all I can understand. I recognize that Your presence in me is a source of power. I thank You that Your Spirit lives in me and is willing to produce in me all the holy qualities You desire. I submit myself to You; I yield myself in the best way I know how; and by faith, right now, I acknowledge the power of the Holy Spirit in my life. I am, therefore, living by Him and walking in Him. In the name of Jesus Christ. AMEN.

Family Relations

CHAPTER 4

A Parable

AT FIRST, CINDERS WAS GLAD he was part of a fire. He saw people come by to warm themselves. He knew the house was cozy because he and the other coals made it cozy. Each day the kettle was placed over him and the others, and they cooked stew while the people of the house waited.

But Cinders got restless. He could see enough of the world outside the fireplace to know there was more. He grew curious about what was behind the door across the room. He overheard people talking of strange things such as "Cold." He wasn't sure, but he thought "Cold" had children called "Snow," "Frost" and "Rain."

"I must find out for myself," muttered Cinders. The others entreated him to stay, but Cinders set out despite their pleas. Before he reached the edge of the hearth, he started to cool — and die. Lacking energy to do anything else, Cinders sat still and alone on the edge of the hearth.

One of the people came by and, seeing Cinders away from the other coals, flicked him back into the fire. "Welcome back," the coals cried. "We're glad you're here! We weren't as good a fire without you."

"It's good to be back," replied Cinders. "I'm not a fire at all without you."

Think about It

How are you like Cinders?

Cinders left the fire because he was lured by curiosity. What are other things that lure people away from fellowship and may cause them to cool off spiritually?

Do you think the fire should have tried to stop Cinders from leaving? Explain.

Brotherly Love

The family bond is love. And God says, "Let brotherly love continue." *(Hebrews 13:1 — KJV)* Loving one another as brothers and sisters in Christ is more than just a tender emotion. It means relating to one another as to your family.

ONE. Take a moment and think of some of the fond memories you have had of your family while you were a child. Write about one or two of the most enjoyable activities that you recall.

One man described one of his memories this way: "As a child, I especially liked Sunday afternoon drives. We would leave Chicago and go to the country and see farms, animals and forests. Usually, we would stop for an ice cream cone. It was a fun experience that always made me feel very warm toward my family and gave me a sense that we were really one unit."

The same man related this experience to having brotherly love in God's family: "The love that I felt when we went on Sunday afternoon rides is similar to my relationships with other Christians today. I have special times with them, enjoying their company and God's creation. The sense of belonging to one another is a real part of my fellowship. I don't have this relationship with everyone in God's family, but there are several with whom I am very close and continue to develop these relationships."

Use one of your memories to describe your relationship with others in your church family.

TWO. Family situations are not always positive. Read about the problem that Joseph had with his brothers in Genesis 37:3-11.

What do you think caused the problem?

How was the problem resolved? *Genesis 45:4-15*

How can you follow the example of Joseph in your church family?

Building Relationships

Close relationships don't happen by accident. They are deliberately built and carefully maintained. Good relationships develop when you apply God's Word to your life. As you grow in the Lord and experience His power in and through you, you will also grow closer to others in God's family.

Family Relations God's Family — 35

THREE. Your relationship as God's child exists because of His forgiving nature. Relationships with people also require generous amounts of forgiveness. What should characterize your forgiveness of others? *Ephesians 4:31,32*

FOUR. When people feel accepted, they reveal their true feelings; and relationships grow stronger. What kind of acceptance should characterize God's family? *Romans 15:5-7*

FIVE. People come to know one another better by communicating beyond just talk about the weather. Good communication results from people "speaking the truth in love." *(Ephesians 4:15)*

Complete the following sentences with thoughts that are meaningful to you:

When there is truth spoken without love . . .

(continued)

When there is "love" without truth ...

When there is truth spoken with love ...

Three important aspects of developing relationships have been considered in the last three questions. The diagram below illustrates how these things come together and cause relationships to deepen.

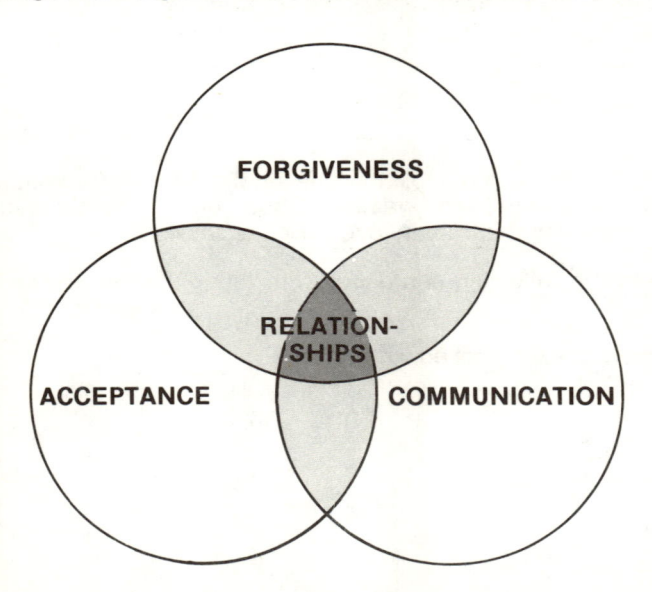

Family Relations   *God's Family — 37*

Church Families

The Scriptures talk of God's family, the Church, in two ways — God's complete family (the universal Church, composed of all believers) and smaller family units called churches (composed of a group of believers gathered in one place).

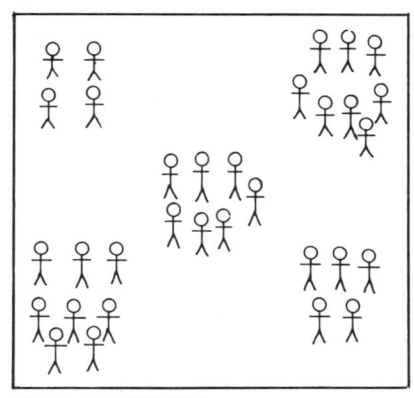

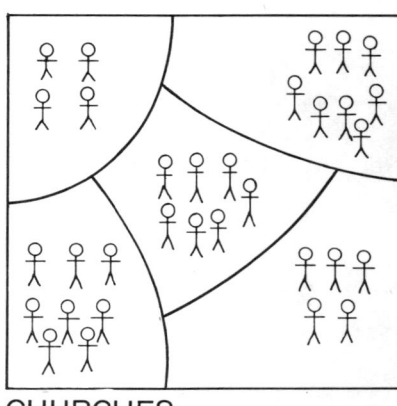

THE CHURCH   CHURCHES

SIX. Paul used family relationships as an example to Timothy when he gave him instructions on leading a church fellowship. Read Paul's instructions in 1 Timothy 5:1,2. Then complete the chart below.

INSTRUCTION TO TIMOTHY	HOW YOU CAN DEMONSTRATE THIS
1.	1.
2.	2.
3.	3.
4.	4.

SEVEN. Jesus told His disciples to "love one another." *(John 13:34)* There are 25 more "one anothers" in the New Testament. Each of these commands can be applied in God's complete family or in a local family unit. What is commanded in each verse below?

I Corinthians 12:25

Ephesians 4:2

Hebrews 3:13

Hebrews 10:24

James 5:16

One way I can fulfill one of those commands in my local fellowship is ...

One way I can fulfill one of those commands beyond my local fellowship to another part of God's family is ...

A Prayerful Response

It is comforting to know that You haven't left me alone in this world. Your presence is a constant source of strength. The others in Your family are a continual encouragement. They really are my brothers and sisters.

I especially thank You for Donna, Gordon, Brenda and Tom. They are so close to me. I love them so much; and I know they love me, too.

Help me be all I ought to be to cause the family spirit to continue to grow at our church. AMEN.

Family Needs

CHAPTER 5

A Parable

ONE DAY, FULL MOON WAS OVERHEARD talking to Distant Star. "I sure am glad I'm not Earth Planet."

Earth Planet felt hurt when he heard it. "What's wrong with me?" he asked.

"Oh, there's nothing wrong with you," replied Moon. "I just wouldn't want to be in your shoes. There are so many needs with all those creatures living on you."

Earth Planet laughed when he heard this and explained how the elements and creatures met the needs of one another. "Rain Drop gives water to Green Plant, Green Plant makes fruits and nuts and vegetables for some of the creatures. They, in turn, do their part."

Full Moon was amazed and fascinated as he listened. "I should have known Majestic Designer would make you complete. He thinks of everything."

"Complete, yes!" replied Earth Planet. "But I always need outside help. If it were not for Bright Sun, the creatures could not function correctly and the needs would not be met."

Think about It

How does the story illustrate meeting needs in God's family?

Who does Bright Sun represent?

What are some ways Earth Planet's "creatures" helping each other are *not* like God's family helping each other?

In what sense is Earth complete in itself? In what sense is it not complete? In what sense is God's family complete in itself? In what sense is it not complete?

Material Needs

ONE. The Book of Acts contains the story of the early Church caring for one another. Read Acts 4:32-35 to see one example of the family meeting needs. What did the family members do to meet one another's needs?

What accompanied this demonstration of love? *Verses 32-34*

TWO. Opportunities for caring abound. One family took the time to get to know one of the older men in their church. Micah was in his eighties. They visited his home and found that his furniture had long passed the "dump" stage, but his small income kept him from replacing it. Micah was thrilled with the gift of a couch and chair.

There are Micahs around you — people on fixed incomes, widows, unemployed and so on. From 2 Corinthians 8:7-15, make a list of reasons to give material aid to others.

THREE. Giving aid to others is not intended to allow them to be irresponsible, but occasionally this problem occurs. How would you apply 2 Thessalonians 3:10-15 to:

People helping others?

People abusing their generosity?

The Church in general?

Inner Needs

When we are deprived of physical necessities, they often become our main concern. Other needs can be just as important, even though they are hidden.

FOUR. What can you do when you have inner needs? *Philippians 4:6,7*

Although this passage does not promise you will receive what you ask for, what does God promise you will receive?

FIVE. Along with the problems Paul mentioned in 2 Corinthians 4:8,9, what inner needs do you think he had?

Why?

Communicating Needs

SIX. Telling God about our needs does not mean we should not talk to others about them also. Instead of being open about their needs, many people hope others will automatically be sensitive to them and help. But openness allows concerned members of the family to become involved. Complete the chart below from 2 Timothy 4:9-17.

WHAT PAUL SAID	WHAT NEED YOU THINK THIS INDICATES

SEVEN. You should make an effort to be aware of people's needs, because they often find it difficult to express them. You can help others be more open by discussing your own needs.

Family Needs

Consider an inner need that you've experienced, and answer these questions:

Did you tell anyone about it?   Yes ☐   No ☐

Did someone help you?   Yes ☐   No ☐

Are you aware of other people having this problem?   Yes ☐   No ☐

If yes, are you helping them?   Yes ☐   No ☐

What insight did this exercise give you about yourself or your church?

When communicating needs to other people, it is easy to slip into depending upon people instead of God. He, alone, is our sufficiency. He has promised to meet "all your needs according to His riches in glory in Christ Jesus." *(Philippians 4:19)* Rely on God and His promises, but don't allow your pride to keep you from communicating with others in God's family. You may miss the blessing God wishes to provide through them.

A Prayerful Response

Thank You, God, for the family. The care, concern and helping hands mean so much to me. Help me be sensitive to those around me and become involved in meeting needs.

When I've gone through many trials, Your peace has sustained me. It is beyond understanding. Give me balance to be free to share needs and to be discreet, also. I recognize that communicating about inner needs can draw me close to others. AMEN.

Family Worship

CHAPTER 6

A Parable

IN A FERTILE VALLEY on the west side of a tall mountain lived Young Pine.

While Young Pine was still a sapling, an owl came to nest in his branches. "I've heard you are a wise creature," said Young Pine. "Can you answer a question I have?"

"I'll try."

Young Pine continued, "I can see blue skies, green forests and snow covered mountains. I can smell perfume from the flowers. I can hear the sounds of countless animals and insects. Who made all these things?"

"God," said Owl.

"Oh," said Young Pine. And he lifted his arms toward Heaven.

Later, an electric storm flashed lightning; and thunder shook the ground. Young Pine shuddered in the violent wind and felt as though he would break in two. When the weather finally calmed, Young Pine asked Owl, "Where does the storm get such power?"

"God," said Owl.

"Wow!" said Young Pine. And he lifted his arms toward Heaven.

The rain washed the mountain and brought food and drink to the forest. "Who gives us this food we're enjoying?"

"God," said Owl.

"I'm glad!" said Young Pine. And he lifted his arms toward Heaven.

Think about It

What three things caused Young Pine to want to worship God?

What causes you to want to worship God?

Young Pine worshipped God by lifting his arms to Him. What are things you do to worship God?

God's Worthiness

People in God's family worship Him in awe and sincerity. This is the kind of worship that comes in response to seeing and understanding God and all of His glory, virtue and worthiness. It is like seeing a fine painting, hearing great music or having other worthwhile experiences. Being exposed to such things brings about a sense of appreciation and words of praise.

When people go through forms of worship without a true sense of God, their words and actions become only empty expressions; and God responds, "Bring your worthless offerings no longer, Their incense is an abomination to Me. New moon and sabbath, the calling of assemblies — I cannot endure iniquity and the solemn assembly. I hate your new moon festivals and your appointed feasts, They have become a burden to Me. I am weary of bearing them." *(Isaiah 1:13,14)*

Being in daily contact with God helps you avoid hollow expressions of worship. As you focus on Him, you will see that He is worthy. Responding to His worthiness is your worship. In fact, the word "worship" was derived from "worthship."

ONE. The Book of Revelation reveals Jesus Christ in His exalted position in Heaven. It tells about people, angels and creatures worshipping Jesus.

The worthiness of Jesus Christ is expressed in many ways in Revelation 4:10,11. Choose an expression describing His worthiness and tell what it means to you.

TWO. The worthiness of God is often considered in two broad areas: Who He is and what He has done. The two passages in the chart below contain many thoughts about these two subjects. Prayerfully read each of these two passages until your heart is moved in appreciation toward God. Briefly write down your thoughts and spend some time worshipping God.

WHO GOD IS	WHAT GOD HAS DONE
Isaiah 40:18-31	Ephesians 1:3-14

Your Worship

THREE. When a Samaritan woman wanted Jesus to tell her the correct location for worshipping God, Jesus said neither the Samaritans' answer nor the Jews' answer was necessary. In other words, externals are not the important part of worshipping God, but internals are. What else did Jesus say about worshipping God in John 4:21-24?

FOUR. The Book of Psalms gives beautiful examples of worship. Reading them can help you in your worship. What actions and attitudes of worship do you see in Psalm 27? Focus on verses 4, 8, 13 and 14.

FIVE. The Psalms give examples of overcoming a major hindrance to worship — being preoccupied with yourself and your problems. King David often complained to God about his plight; and while honestly telling God his feelings, a change would take place in him. Read Psalm 13 and describe the difference you see between the first four and the last two verses of the Psalm.

FIRST FOUR VERSES	LAST TWO VERSES

If you have had the experience of coming to God to tell Him about your problems and He changed your focus to look at Him and His glory, briefly describe it.

Worshipping Together

SIX. Many of the Psalms were written to be read responsively. Reading them aloud is one way to have meaningful worship with believers. Other elements of worshipping God are praise, thanksgiving, music and celebrating the Lord's Supper.

Why do you think praise is called a sacrifice in Hebrews 13:15?

What causes music to be worship? *Ephesians 5:18,19*

Family Worship   **God's Family — 55**

Why should you celebrate the Lord's Supper? *1 Corinthians 11:23-26*

SEVEN. Our worship of God is not primarily for our enjoyment. It is an offering to God. But we should have a meaningful time when we worship. What has been done in a worship service that was particularly meaningful to you?

What do you think must be true of your life to keep group worship meaningful?

A Prayerful Response

You are God — great, mighty and awesome. When I consider Your works, I am stunned. You created the world and all that is in it with one word. I think of Your power when I feel the sun or see the mountains or hear thunder.

When I consider all You have done for me, I feel so fortunate. You came to earth as a man to die for me. You've made me Your child. You've forgiven me and given to me.

And when I think that the great God who has done all this lives in me, I praise You and thank You. Thank You for loving me. I love You, too. AMEN.

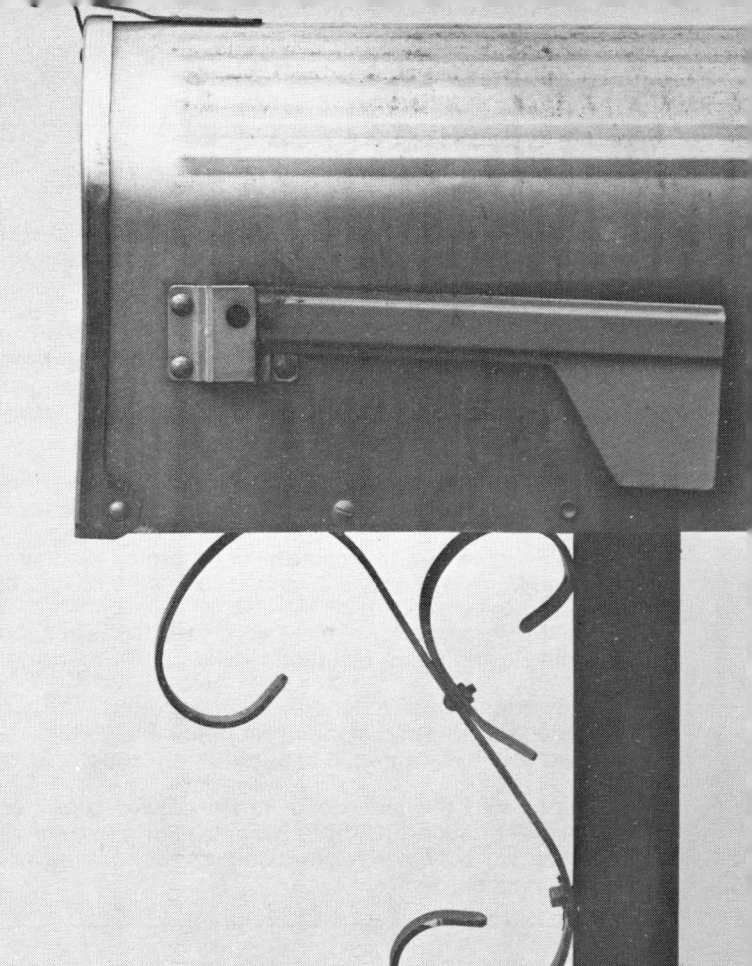

Family House

CHAPTER 7

A Parable

WHEN THE FLOWERS and other plants first saw it, they thought it was just metal and glass. So, when many of them were taken inside, those left behind were confused.

But they soon learned it was a greenhouse. They heard all about the controlled temperature and lighting and moisture. The structure even had a seedling room, rooting room and grafting area. "What a wonderful idea," they thought. "We would surely be a better garden if we had a greenhouse, too."

All the plants agreed that they wanted a greenhouse. Soon the entire garden was organized to work on the project.

When the gardener came by one morning to admire the flowers, he found Morning Glory still closed. "What's wrong?" he asked.

"We were up late last night working on the Greenhouse Planning Committee, and so we just didn't wake up this morning."

Next, he went to smell Rose and found no fragrance. Rose explained she was part of the greenhouse Fund-Raising Committee and had sold her fragrance to a perfume company to earn money.

Alarmed, the gardener called the flowers together. "It's fine to want a greenhouse, and there are many things we can do with one," he explained; "but *having* a greenhouse must never be more important than *being* a garden."

Think about It

What do the flowers represent?

What is a spiritual parallel to owning a greenhouse? to being a garden?

What is the difference between the flowers and plants in the greenhouse and a garden? How does that illustrate a church?

What are some good reasons for wanting to own a "greenhouse?"

What are some good reasons for not wanting to own one?

The Tabernacle

The first building used for the worship of God was the *tabernacle*. It was not a permanent building, but a tent-like structure built by the Israelites under Moses' direction according to the plan God gave him. The tabernacle was central to their worship and was moved with them to each new camping site.

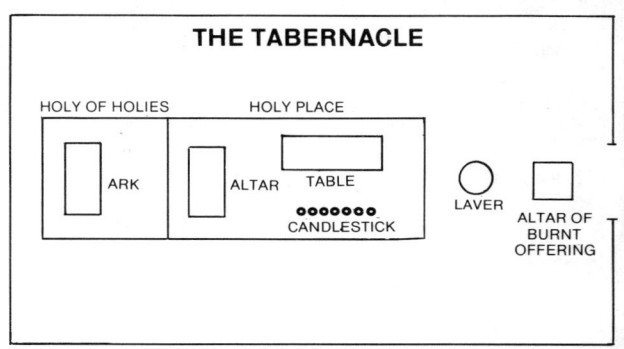

THE TABERNACLE

HOLY OF HOLIES | HOLY PLACE
ARK | ALTAR TABLE
  | ●●●●●●● CANDLESTICK
LAVER ALTAR OF BURNT OFFERING

ONE. The tabernacle consisted of two main parts, the Holy Place and the Holy of Holies. Read Exodus 40:33-38 and explain why the tabernacle was holy.

The Old Temple

TWO. About 400 years after the tabernacle was built, David was King of Israel. The tabernacle no longer existed, and most of its furnishings had been lost. David wanted to build a permanent house for God and began to amass materials for it, but God did not allow David to build it. Instead, Solomon, his son and successor to the throne, built it. This building was called the *temple*. How do we know that the temple was as holy as the tabernacle? *Haggai 1:8, 2:9*

THREE. Actually, there was more than one temple, as through age, wars and disasters, successive temples were destroyed or partially destroyed and rebuilt. By the time of Jesus, the temple had changed. Read Matthew 23:37-39.

The temple had been called the House of God, but Jesus called it ... *verse 38*

The temple had been holy, but Jesus said it was ... *verse 38*

The New Temple

FOUR. The tabernacle is gone and the temple desolate; what has replaced them? *1 Corinthians 3:16*

Use 1 Corinthians 6:19,20 to complete the following diagram.

MAIN POINT
Your body is _____

SUPPORTING FACTS:

_____ is in you.

You are not _____.

You have been _____.

APPLICATION

THEREFORE,

Family House   **God's Family — 61**

FIVE. Being the "temple of God" is a great responsibility. Complete the chart below.

VERSE	WHAT DOES IT SAY ABOUT "THE TEMPLE"?	WHAT IS ONE IMPLICATION OF THIS STATEMENT FOR TODAY?
1 Corinthians 3:17		
2 Corinthians 6:16-18		

Buildings

SIX. Since each person in God's family is God's temple, there is no specific place or building needed for worshipping God. What are some of the places Christians gathered for worship and for teaching in the first century?

Acts 1:13,14

Acts 20:20

Colossians 4:15

SEVEN. Today, most family groups (local churches) own a building to use for teaching, worship and other functions. These buildings are usually called "churches." This may confuse people as they read the Bible. "Church" in the Bible *always* refers to people — either all the people in God's family or a small part of them.

THE PLACE WHERE "TEMPLES" MEET

(continued)

	GOD'S "TEMPLE" TODAY	CHURCH BUILDINGS
From what you learned in this study, list the differences between God's "temple" today and church buildings.		
In light of these differences, what should be your attitude toward each?		

A Prayerful Response

Oh, Father, how can it be that I am Your temple? What a high calling! Me — Your house! You could have the finest palace with gold and silver inlaid with pearl and ivory. Yet You choose to live in me. I am unworthy.

Help me to remember this great privilege so I will keep Your temple holy, clean and ready for Your service.

Lord, I thank You for the local church. It gives me fellowship, guidance and support. I also thank You for your facilities. They make it easier to do many things. Help us keep them properly maintained without switching our affection from You and from one another to brick and mortar. AMEN.

Family Conflict

CHAPTER 8

A Parable

SQUIRRELS SCAMPERED, BIRDS DARTED and rabbits streaked — all because of the ear-splitting, brain-jarring, ground-shaking noise.

Across the meadow, two rams were charging one another in combat. Refusing to yield, each held his ground and continued thrusting with lowered head. Each time, their horns would meet with a new crash.

"Why?" asked Rabbit. "I don't know," replied Squirrel. "There's plenty of room and food for everyone."

"I'm scared," chirped Baby Robin. Mrs. Redbreast comforted her child, "It will be over soon. I hope."

Finally, it stopped. Exhausted and hurt, one ram retreated into the forest. The victor's wounds glistened in the sunlight. Peace returned to the mountain and the valleys.

Think about It

Does anyone here know why rams butt heads? How is that like what people do?

The other animals were disturbed by the butting. How do you react when you are near tension between two people?

What do you think are the main reasons tension can exist between people in God's family?

Disunity

ONE. Whenever there is bad will, hurt feelings, arguments, bitterness or mere indifference, there is lack of unity. Why is unity in the church family so important?

Matthew 18:19,20

(continued)

Family Conflict

John 17:21-23

TWO. Usually, members of God's family don't show disunity by being openly hostile. The indications are more subtle. What indications of a break in unity are given in 1 Corinthians 1:12?

What do you think caused the people to make these various statements?

What would be a similar situation that might occur today?

"I, therefore, the prisoner of the Lord, entreat you to walk in a manner worthy of the calling with which you have been called, with all humility and gentleness, with patience, showing forbearance to one another in love, being diligent to preserve the unity of the Spirit in the bond of peace. There is one body and one Spirit. Just as also you were called in one hope of your calling; one Lord, one faith, one baptism, one God and Father of all who is over all and through all and in all." Ephesians 4:1-6

FOUNDATION FOR UNITY

Curing Disunity

THREE. Many times disunity results because someone feels another person has treated him or her badly. If someone in God's family hurts you, what can you do to turn this situation into an opportunity for improving your relationship and "win" him? *Matthew 18:15*

Expecting the best response from the other person shows love and trust. But what should you do if he isn't "won"? *Matthew 18:16,17*

How does this procedure contribute to solving disunity?

FOUR. Read Galatians 6:1. If there is a problem in your local church, who should handle it?

How should it be handled?

Family Conflict **God's Family — 67**

FIVE. When you try to solve a problem of disunity, people in the family will usually respond positively if you communicate with them honestly and lovingly. At other times, a root cause of disunity needs to be dealt with. Choose one of the problem situations listed below, and write in a cause and a solution from the passages.

EVIDENCE OF DISUNITY	CAUSE	SOLUTION
STRIFE	*1 Corinthians 3:1-4*	*Galatians 5:16*
SUPERIORITY & INFERIORITY	*2 Corinthians 10:12*	*Philippians 2:3,4*
CIVIL SUITS	*1 Corinthians 6:7,8*	*Colossians 3:12-14*

Handling Tension

SIX. Unity in God's family does not mean sameness. God created you individually and made you different from others. His family includes people from every culture and society. Variety of backgrounds means there are often different ideas. Even differing ideas do not need to create disharmony. What should you do to maintain unity with people in God's family when you disagree with them on an issue? *Romans 14:1-6*

SEVEN. Give your opinion of this statement about differing ideas: "In essentials, unity — in non-essentials, liberty — in all things, love."

Take a moment to reflect on your relationships with others in God's family. Without writing answers, ask yourself, "Have I done or said anything that hurt someone? Do I need to apologize or correct a problem?"

If you answer, "yes," follow the directions of Matthew 5:23,24 to re-establish unity.

Then ask yourself, "Has someone hurt me? Am I angry about something that someone has done?"

If you answer, "yes," then first fulfill your responsibility given in Ephesians 4:31,32. Then follow the direction of Matthew 18:15 if you still feel there is tension.

A Prayerful Response

Thank You for all the oneness I have with You and the rest of Your family. Being in a family that is together in heart has always been a deep desire of mine.

I must confess that I don't always feel at one with every person in my church. I need Your strength to be forgiving and understanding. I know that at times I'm at fault. I need to be more loving and more sensitive. There are other times when I really think others are causing a problem. When I think of talking to them, I get scared. Is it really my place to confront them? Help me to know. Give me the wisdom and strength to do what You want me to do. AMEN.

Later ...

I can hardly believe it, God! When I talked to Phil about what he was doing that irritated others, he appreciated it. He didn't know why people were reacting to him, and he wants to be kind and loving. Thank You for such a great brother. AMEN.

MARY
7-30-81

CHRISTIAN
11-23-80

ALEX
JAN-1-80

MARY
JAN-1-80

CHRISTIAN
2-1-79

CHRISTIAN
1-23-78

Family Goal

CHAPTER 9

A Parable

IT WAS IMPOSSIBLE TO DETERMINE who started it, but soon all of the lemmings* were moving — walking, trotting, running.

Leonard found himself in the frenzy of activity, and he wished he could see how to stop it. But he kept running.

"Why are we running?" he panted between strides. Those near him showed by their glares that it was wrong to ask. So he kept running.

Later, as his confidence returned, Leonard tried again. "Where are we going?"

"East," said one.

"I don't know," said another.

"To the sea!" added a third.

Leonard was still confused. But he kept running.

*Small arctic rodents. The European species engages in recurrent mass migration which often ends by drowning in the ocean.

Think about It

What are lemmings and what do they do?

How are people something like lemmings?

If you have ever had the experience of trying to get answers to life's questions when no one seemed to understand you, describe it.

What should you do if you feel you are just running and not accomplishing anything?

The Commission

ONE. God has given His family a goal so each person can have direction in life. No one must be a lemming, plunging into a sea of confusion.

Family Goal   *God's Family — 73*

The family goal is stated in the Great Commission which was given by Jesus Christ after He was crucified and rose from the dead. It is not called the Great Commission because it is more important than other commissions. It is called "great" because it is a command that captures the essence of all Jesus wants the Church to accomplish. Use the statement of the Commission in Matthew 28:18-20 to complete the diagram below.

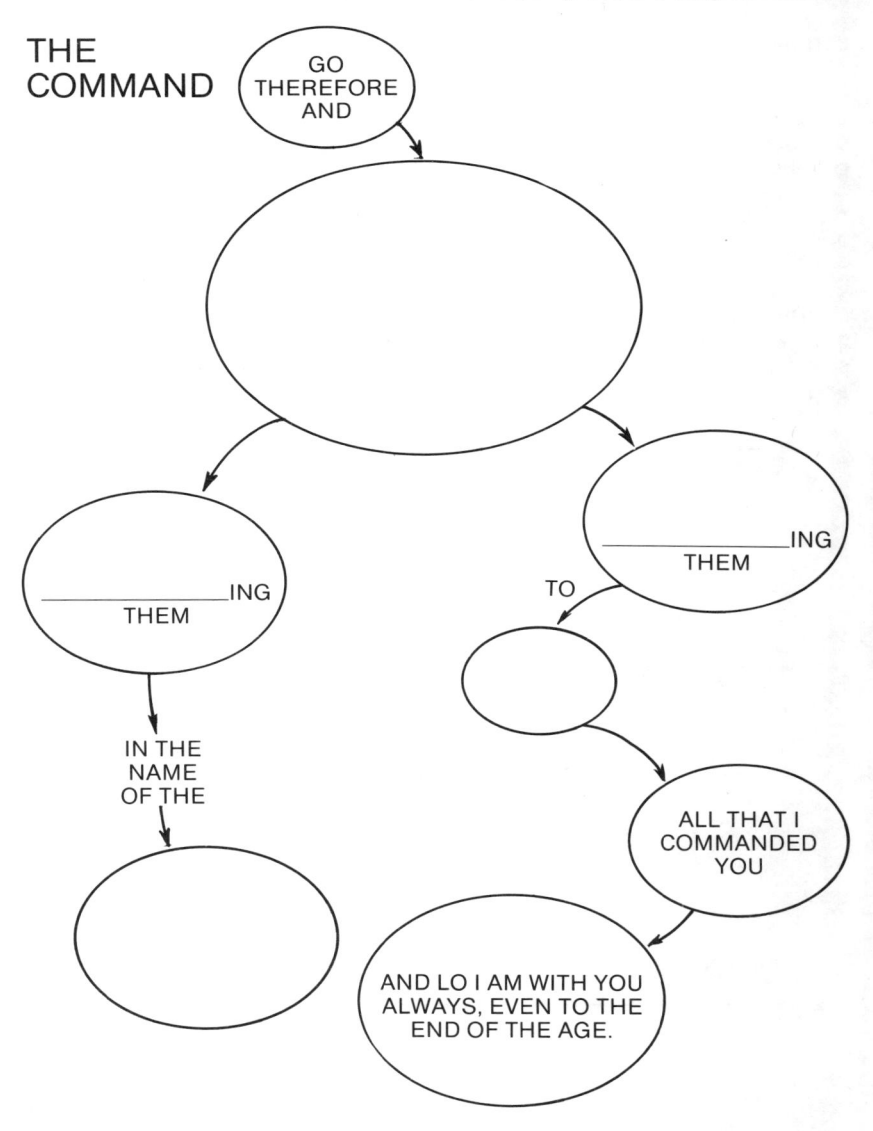

THE COMMAND

- GO THEREFORE AND
  - _____
    - _____ING THEM
      - IN THE NAME OF THE
        - _____
    - _____ING THEM
      - TO _____
        - ALL THAT I COMMANDED YOU
          - AND LO I AM WITH YOU ALWAYS, EVEN TO THE END OF THE AGE.

TWO. The command of the Great Commission is to "make disciples of all nations." From your chart on the previous page you can see that making disciples has two primary actions — baptizing and teaching to obey.

Throughout the history of the Church, baptism has been seen as a public declaration of trust in Jesus Christ as one's Lord and Savior. So, "baptizing," in the Great Commission, is more than water and more than a ceremony; it culminates the evangelistic efforts of the family.

"Teaching them to obey" is the second major action in the Great Commission. This is more than education and more than information. It is developing obedience to all of Jesus' commands. This submission to Him produces spiritual growth.

So, to "make disciples," the family must emphasize both evangelism and obedience which produces growth.

If people get these two emphases out of balance, they get caught in one of two dilemmas. A person over-involved in outreach is like the man on the left — weak and impoverished. A person who only takes in spiritual food without any outreach is pictured on the right — encumbered and slow.

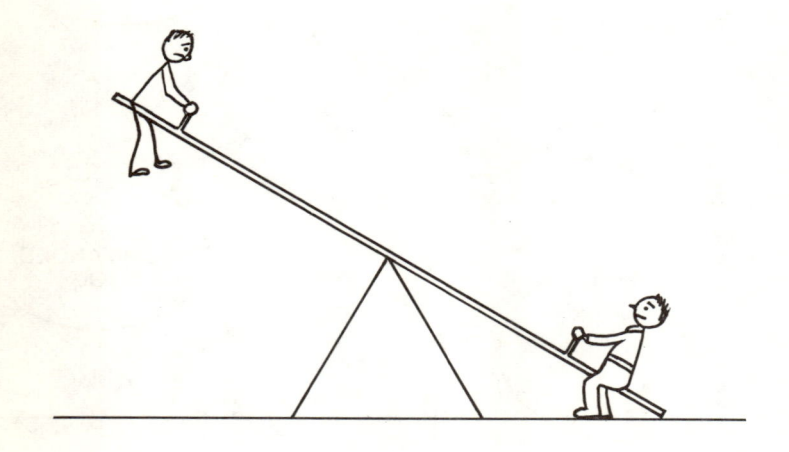

Family Goal

Complete the chart below by writing in the "taking in" and "giving out" actions indicated by the verses.

VERSES	TAKING IN	GIVING OUT
Acts 1:8		
2 Timothy 3:16,17		
1 John 1:3		

Jesus' Disciples

THREE. The Great Commission was not a new thought. It was consistent with Jesus' ministry throughout His life. Matthew 4:18-20 tells about Jesus recruiting two disciples. What did He ask them to do?

What result did He promise? *Verse 19*

How do you consider this statement similar to the Great Commission?

FOUR. When Jesus talked about the Church for the first time, He pictured it as an army attacking the gates of hell.

In Jesus' day, an army wanting to attack a city usually centered its forces on the gate. If the defenses held, it was said that the gate prevailed or overcame. If the defenses failed, the gate did not prevail; and the attacking army won.

What does Jesus' statement indicate about the efforts of His Church? *Matthew 16:18.*

FIVE. Jesus gave a major portion of His time and effort to His disciples. They lived with Him, and He taught them and trained them. What conditions did Jesus set for being His disciple? *Luke 9:23-26*

Being a Disciple

SIX. Jesus sets high standards for people to be His disciples because He expects His disciples to reflect Him to the world. List the marks of a disciple from each reference below, and then complete the chart.

VERSES	MARK OF A DISCIPLE	A SPECIFIC ACTION THAT DEMONSTRATES THIS QUALITY
John 8:31		
John 13:34,35		
John 15:8		

Family Goal

SEVEN. You have seen that Jesus expects His Church to be making disciples as He commanded. How has your church contributed to your growth as a disciple?

Look over your answers to this chapter. Based on your understanding of discipleship, what do you think is the next major step you need for your growth as a disciple of Jesus Christ?

A Prayerful Response

Lord, I really want to be Your disciple. There are times, when I look at my life, that I feel disqualified. I'm not sure that I've forsaken everything for You. On the other hand, I do see growth in myself. You've made me much more loving and kind. I praise You for this because this love *in* me is not *from* me.

Help me, God, to discipline myself. I need to spend time in Your Word and prayer, and it doesn't always come easily. As Your disciple, I want to reach out to others with the gospel. Specifically, I would like to talk to Kevin about You. Open an opportunity, and give me words to speak.

Thank You for Tom and the Sunday School class. It really helps me a lot. AMEN.

Family Team
CHAPTER 10

A Parable

"I'LL NEVER AMOUNT TO ANYTHING as a small black ant," thought Anthony. "I'll become something better."

He spied a group of grasshoppers. "I'll be a great jumper!" thought Anthony. Though he tried repeatedly, he couldn't get off the ground. His efforts only made the grasshoppers laugh.

"I'll learn to spin a web," thought Anthony, "and weave beautiful designs." He took web classes, changed his diet and even tried self-hypnosis. Nothing worked.

Dejected, he returned to the ant hill. "Come on!" called one of the foremen. "You're just in time to help move this piece of bread into storage!"

"It's bigger than a thousand of us," thought Anthony, as he came to help. "We'll never be able to do it."

All day, the army of ants cut off crumbs and carried them to store in the hill. By evening, the piece of bread was safely inside. "I wouldn't have believed it if I hadn't seen it!" Anthony exclaimed. "Together we did the impossible." And Anthony was proud to be an ant.

Think about It

In what ways is God's family like an army of ants?

In what ways is God's family different from an army of ants?

If you have ever had feelings like Anthony, would you please describe them?

Can you give an illustration of how teamwork has accomplished "the impossible"?

Teamwork

When Jesus gave the family goal of making disciples, He did not expect any one person to do it all. He expected His disciples to cooperate.

Family Team   *God's Family —*

Today we are in a much larger family, but He still wants us to work together toward accomplishing this goal.

ONE. By the words used to describe the family, the Bible indicates that teamwork is needed. Two biblical pictures used for the family are listed below. Below each, explain one way this term indicates a need for teamwork.

AN ARMY	A BODY

TWO. One reason teamwork is needed to accomplish our goal is that no one has all the abilities it takes to make disciples. God has given us different gifts which are all needed. One explanation for spiritual gifts and their use is in 1 Corinthians 12.

Why has God given gifts to all Christians? *verse 7*

Who decides which gift(s) you have? *verse 11*

What are some gifts mentioned in this chapter?

> **THREE.** The variety of gifts should not divide the family into parts, but are given so we can accomplish more through cooperation. Show the relationship between unity and variety by completing the chart below from 1 Corinthians 12:4-6.

There are differences of ...	... but the same ...
1.	
2.	
3.	

Team Goal

FOUR. The diagram illustrates what can happen when gifts are viewed as an end in themselves. They become turned in on themselves, and they miss the objective of making disciples.

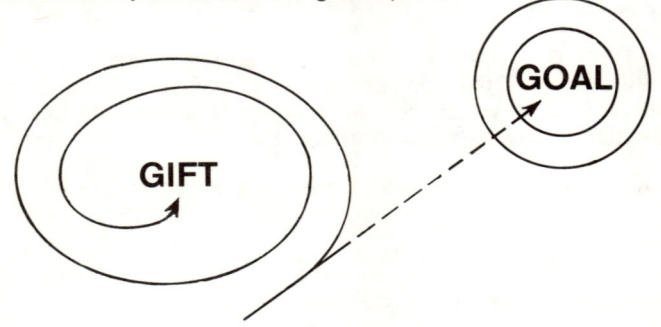

The church at Corinth had problems with people exercising their gifts properly. What contributed to this problem? *1 Corinthians 3:3*

What attitudes will keep you from being turned in on yourself? *Ephesians 4:1-3*

Family Team   *God's Family — 83*

FIVE. The diagram shows all the gifts working together to make disciples. All the gifts are focused on the family goal. Read about this process in Ephesians 4:11-16.

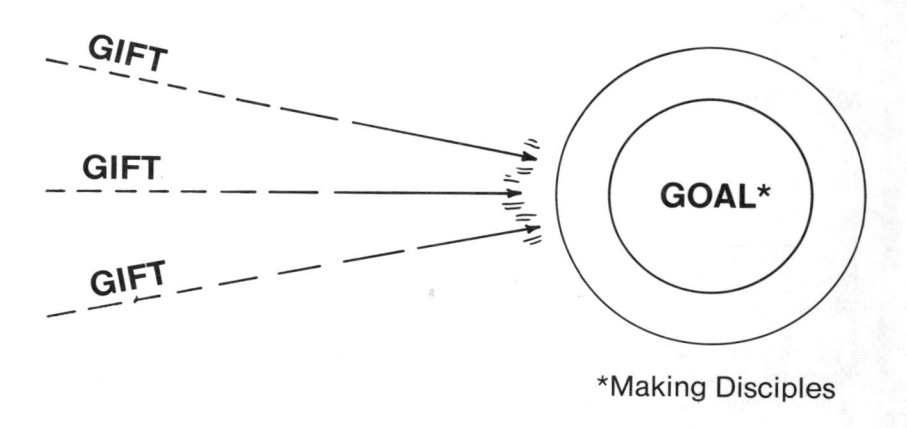

GIFT

GIFT

GIFT

GOAL*

*Making Disciples

What does this passage say about cooperating with one another?

What happens when gifts work together to make disciples? *Verse 16*

Team Members

SIX. When gifts are used correctly, people are sensitive to one another and good relationships result. Read 1 Corinthians 12:22-26.

Why should you care when another person in the family is suffering?

Why do you think there is indifference at times?

SEVEN. Romans 12:3 says you should have a realistic and sober evaluation of yourself. This means you should not overestimate or underestimate your value.

A person underestimating his value might say, "I can't do as much as others, so I guess I'm not much use." What statement in 1 Corinthians 12:15-21 corresponds to this statement?

How is it shown to be wrong?

A person overestimating himself might say, "I don't need others, I can do it myself." What statement in 1 Corinthians 12:15-21 corresponds to this statement?

How is it shown to be wrong?

Family Team   *God's Family — 85*

The diagram below illustrates how different people with different gifts "fit" together to form a church. Follow the example by filling in the names of people in your church along with one gift for each.

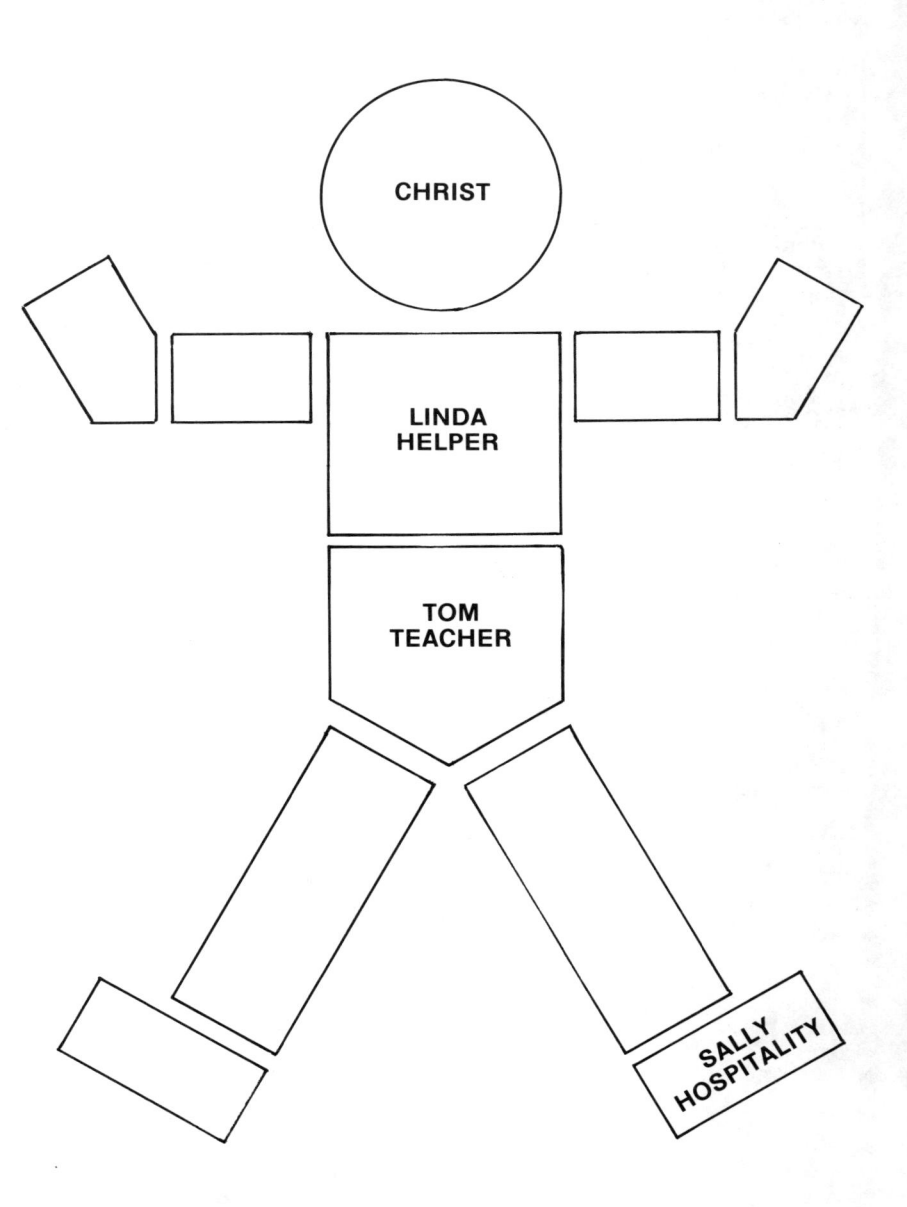

A Prayerful Response

Thank You for the family and all the differences we have. I see more clearly than ever that I need people who are different from me. I am pleased to know they also need me. I look to You to strengthen me and empower me so I can do my share.

Sometimes I feel that I am working alone. I don't sense the rest of the team. When I feel this way, help me to remember the others. People like Tom, George, Linda and Rick — they really mean a lot to me. Thank You for them. Thank You also for the rest who may not be helping me personally but are still part of the team.

Help me to have a proper perspective of myself. There are times I am prideful and think too much of myself. Then I sometimes think I can do nothing, which is out of balance in the other direction. Give me Your perspective. AMEN.

Family Leaders

CHAPTER 11

A Parable

WAYLON WOLF CONSTANTLY GRUMBLED about how he didn't like the pack leader. But really, Waylon didn't like to take orders. He wanted to make decisions for himself.

One day, while the rest of the pack was napping, Waylon slipped away to make it on his own. Soon he came upon a fallen pine tree in a clearing. The needles were dry and soft, and Waylon decided it wasn't important to dig out an elaborate den. Instead, he curled up in the soft needles near the trunk and finished his nap.

As he slept, it clouded and began to rain. Waylon began to get wet and couldn't sleep any longer. He decided to hunt for some food.

Without the help of the others, Waylon realized he must rule out feasting on elk or deer. Instead, he tracked and killed a small gray rodent. It tasted terrible to Waylon, and he ate very little. He began to understand why the pack leader snarled whenever someone suggested hunting small game.

Later, Waylon decided to scout a territory that the pack leader had always avoided. As he rounded a clump of trees, Waylon startled a huge bear that was eating berries. It took the last of Waylon's strength to outrun and hide from the bear.

Tired, hungry and ashamed, Waylon returned to the pack.

Think about It

What are ways people are like Waylon?

What kinds of decisions do people like to make for themselves?

What are advantages that you enjoy from having leaders?

Requirements for Leaders

ONE. God has provided leaders to direct, feed and protect His family. Leaders are not better people than other family members, nor are they more important to God. But their decisions affect many other people,

Family Leaders — God's Family — 89

so there are special requirements for them.

Paul listed several requirements for leaders when he told Titus to appoint them in Crete. From Titus 1:6-9, summarize in one or two sentences requirements for each area listed below.

LEADER'S FAMILY	LEADER'S REPUTATION	LEADER'S ABILITIES

TWO. In the reference above, Paul listed requirements for a leader's family first as though it were uppermost in his mind. Why do you think it is important for a leader to have correct relationships at home?

Instructions for Leaders

THREE. Leaders in God's family have greater responsibilities than other family members. Paul wrote to Timothy about his responsibilities as a pastor, giving him instructions for leading the church. What instructions are given in 2 Timothy 4:1-5? Put a check mark by each instruction you think applies only to a leader.

What can you do to help your leaders fulfill one of these responsibilities?

FOUR. Church leaders also make a commitment to people. What does 2 Corinthians 12:14,15 indicate about the extent of this commitment?

In your own words, describe what happens when leaders aren't committed to their people. *John 10:12,13*

FIVE. In 1 Peter 5:1-3, Peter also compares leaders and the rest of the family to shepherds and sheep. List the commands he gives to leaders, and explain what you think these commands mean.

How should you respond to the direction of your leaders? *1 Peter 5:5*

What kind of relationship is needed between leaders and the rest of the family so people will respond properly to one another?

92 – God's Family

Results of Good Leading

SIX. When leaders fulfill their responsibilities, people are helped and new leaders are developed. In 2 Timothy 2:2, Paul describes this "chain" of emerging leaders.

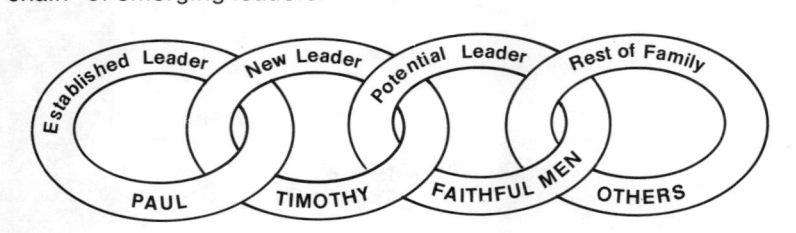

Established Leader — PAUL
New Leader — TIMOTHY
Potential Leader — FAITHFUL MEN
Rest of Family — OTHERS

Read 2 Timothy 2:2 and answer the following questions.

What had Paul done?

What was Timothy to do?

What should "faithful men" do?

Which one of the four links best describes you?

SEVEN. As leaders fulfill their responsibilities and relationships are healthy, a chain of events takes place. Complete the chain diagram from Ephesians 4:11,12.

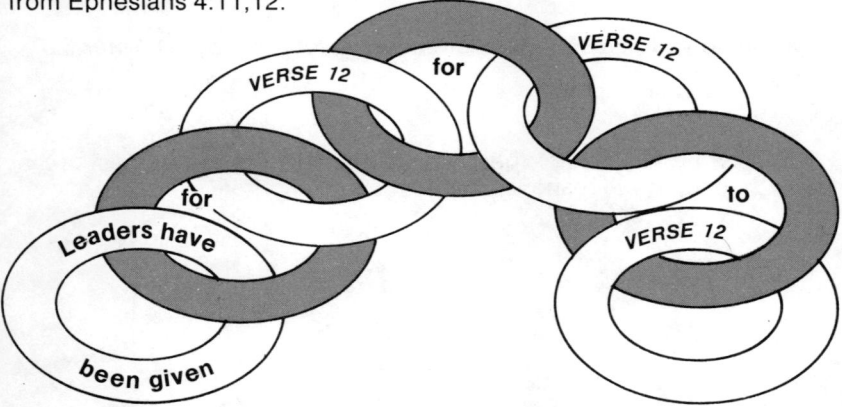

Leaders have been given / for / VERSE 12 / for / VERSE 12 / to / VERSE 12

Each link in the preceding chain is dependent upon the previous link. Leaders do not directly complete the work of the ministry. It is their job to equip you so you can do it.

A Prayerful Response

Thank You, Lord, for my spiritual leaders — for Pastor King, for Ron, for Tom and several others. I've appreciated them for a long time, but this study has helped me understand the great responsibility they have. I really want to help them do a good job of leading our church. I commit myself to supporting them.

God, what do You want me to do about being a leader? I've been asked to take some responsibility, but I'm in a quandary. I don't fully meet all the qualifications You set down — but I guess no one except Jesus has completely met them all. Maybe I've been using this as an excuse for laziness. I'm willing to take the job; but I'll need Your power, and I'll need some training from the church leaders.

Thank You for the opportunity to serve. AMEN.

Family Commitment

CHAPTER 12

A Parable

ALTHOUGH HORACE WAS A HORNET, he admired bees. He admired them so much that he completed an application to join the local beehive.

"Although this is highly irregular," said the interviewing bee, "the Queen thinks an exchange program may be good. All we need to do is find the correct position for you."

"I'll do anything," said Horace.

"There are three positions open," the interviewer continued "— hive worker, pollen collector and guard."

"What does the hive worker do?"

"A hive worker constructs new honeycombs for incoming nectar, caps the full cells and takes care of odd jobs around the hive."

"Doesn't it get hot in here in the summertime?"

"Oh, yes, that's another one of your jobs — air conditioning. When it gets too hot inside, the workers must go to the opening and fan their wings to cool the hive."

"This sounds too hard," Horace thought to himself. "What about becoming a pollen collector?" he asked. "I'd be able to fly around and enjoy the outdoors, right?"

"Not exactly. You must collect nectar from flowers. At times you'll have to fly miles to find it. Once you find it, you must carry a full load."

Horace thought this sounded like back-breaking effort, so he asked about becoming a guard.

"A guard's life is easy. He does nothing — that is, nothing until an intruder appears. Then he must attack the intruder, stinging him until he retreats."

"But," said Horace, "don't you die once you have lost your stinger?"

"Of course, but it is necessary for the good of the hive."

The interviewer glanced down at his clipboard to see if he had left out anything. When he looked up, Horace was gone.

Family Commitment *God's Family — 97*

Think about It

Why do you think Horace decided not to try to be a bee?

What commitments would Horace have had to make to become a bee?

How is a beehive like God's family?

Commitment to God

ONE. God created the family for you to enjoy, but He expects you to make a commitment also — a commitment to Him, to the family and its leaders. The first commitment to make is to God. You don't make a commitment to Him so He will do something for you. You make your commitment because He *has* done so much for you.

Seeing what God has done for you should cause you to present your body to Him as a living sacrifice according to Romans 12:1,2. Use the concepts in these verses to complete the diagram below.

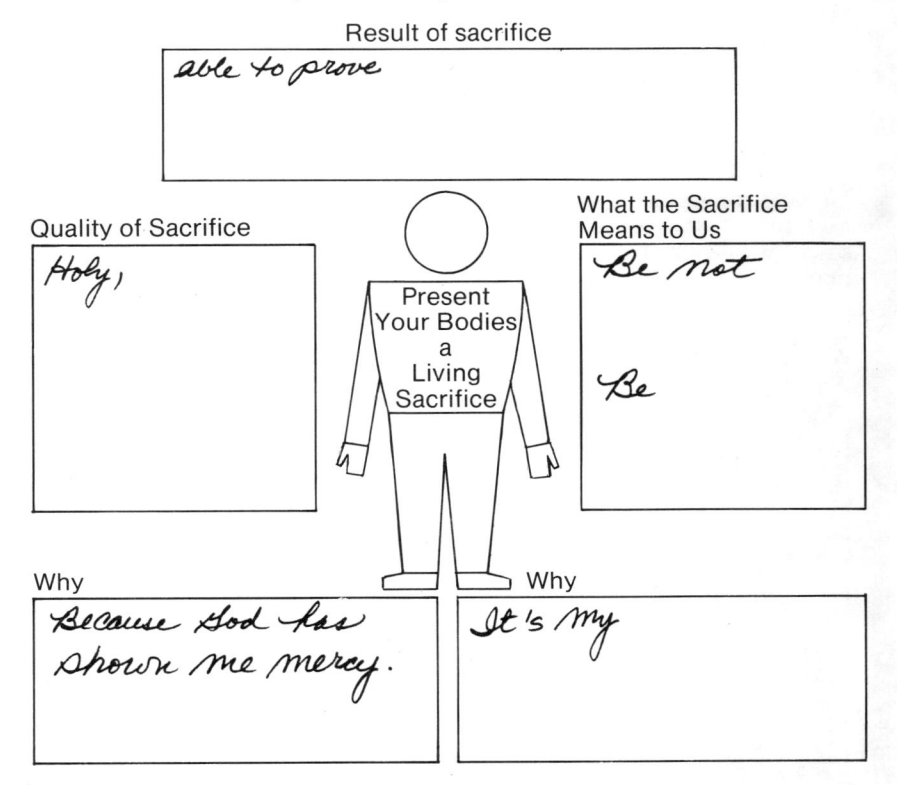

Result of sacrifice: *able to prove*

Quality of Sacrifice: *Holy,*

Present Your Bodies a Living Sacrifice

What the Sacrifice Means to Us: *Be not* / *Be*

Why: *Because God has shown me mercy.*

Why: *It's my*

Select one of the segments from the diagram on the previous page and tell what it means to you.

TWO. Jesus did not hesitate to ask people to make commitments to Him. He insisted that those who were not willing to commit themselves were not worthy of Him. What did Jesus tell His followers to do? *Luke 9:23*

How do you think Jesus wants us to apply that today?

THREE. A commitment to God includes a commitment to people He puts in positions of authority. "Let every person be in subjection to the governing authorities. For there is no authority except from God, and those which exist are established by God." *(Romans 13:1)* What two commitments did the people in Macedonia make? *2 Corinthians 8:5*

What does commitment to church leaders include? *1 Thessalonians 5:12,13*

Why should you commit yourself to church leaders? *Hebrews 13:17*

Family Commitment   *God's Family — 99*

Commitment to the Family

FOUR. One way you show love toward God is showing love and commitment to the rest of the family. "If someone says, 'I love God,' and hates his brother, he is a liar, for the one who does not love his brother whom he has seen, cannot love God whom he has not seen." *(1 John 4:20)*

What are some of the things that will happen when the members of God's family are committed to one another?

1 CORINTHIANS 12:26,27	1 TIMOTHY 5:3-8
HEBREWS 13:1-3	JAMES 5:13-16

FIVE. Jesus, Himself, is our example of love. He said, "A new commandment I give to you, that you love one another, even as I have loved you, that you also love one another. By this all men will know that you are My disciples, if you have love for one another." *(John 13:34,35)* In the chart below, list some specific examples of His love and one way you can follow each example.

SPECIFIC EXAMPLE OF LOVE	WAY TO FOLLOW THIS EXAMPLE
He fed the 5000	I can help feed hungry people.

Evaluating Your Commitment

SIX. How can you evaluate your commitment? *Matthew 6:21*

SEVEN. Take some time to review the twelve lessons in this book. From your study, what three benefits of being in God's family are most important to you?

1.

2.

3.

What commitments to God's family do you need to make in order to preserve these benefits?

What contribution can you make so these benefits can be enjoyed by others in God's family?

A Prayerful Response

I am Yours, Lord. Do what You wish with me. You've been so good to me. I cannot do anything less than to give You myself. People around me want me to be like they are, but I want to be different because You control me. I am willing to pay any price to fulfill Your will for me.

Thank You for the family. I love them. Special thanks for our local "branch" — my church. They are great. I want to give to them, help them, encourage them and support them. I hereby commit my time, my talents and my treasure to my church.

In the name of Jesus Christ and without reservations. AMEN.

Other Discipling Helps from Churches Alive

Churches Alive

The Church is the heart of God's plan for fulfilling our Lord's Great Commission, "Go therefore and make disciples . . ." With that basic conviction, the ministry of Churches Alive was launched. We help churches gain a basic understanding of the biblical concepts for discipling and then implement a solid discipling ministry of their own.

Churches Alive staff are currently working with both large and small churches of approximately 35 denominational and independent backgrounds. Their experience in the areas of discipleship and evangelism enables churches to move ahead with confidence while avoiding costly mistakes.

Once a church has adopted the priorities for disciplemaking, we offer a plan which enables it to accomplish its goals. The plan, "Growing by Discipling," is founded on the fact that every church has a God-given resource — a core of people with whom a solid, purposeful ministry of discipleship can be started.

Growing by Discipling allows churches to begin with the staff, lay leaders and facilities they now have to develop a discipling ministry that meets the needs of Christians of all ages, backgrounds and stages of maturity.

There are three ways Churches Alive serves churches —

Consultants

A staff consultant assists a church to develop a long-range discipleship plan. He usually works with the church for several years to assure that the discipling plan is on a sure footing and is producing results.

"Our consultant has certainly made good use of his many years of experience in discipleship ministries. We are grateful for his insights, his perception of needs in our congregation and his suggestions which often help us take the necessary steps as we plan for future ministries. We are thankful for the way Churches Alive has helped our church to get on track and keep us moving in the right direction through accountability to our consultant."
— California Pastor

Training Conferences

Church leaders may take advantage of both basic and continuing training in Growing by Discipling at various locations throughout the year.

"This conference has given me more encouragement in my ministry

than I have experienced since I entered it. It has prodded me into developing long-range plans for our church, as well as beginning to train leaders."
— *Minnesota Growing by Discipling Institute Attendee*

Materials

Churches Alive provides a full complement of materials to launch and continue a church's discipling ministry. Included are leaders' guides, study materials and training tapes.

". . . I have not seen anything being published that even approaches that which is being done by Churches Alive. They are striking at several of the really needy areas in the church — leadership, fellowship, controlled Bible study, prayer and evangelism. The results that I have seen in this church and in several other churches have convinced me that this is something that our churches need to work into their programs."
— *Pennsylvania Christian Publisher*

The following pages contain information about materials that will help you evaluate and launch an effective Growing by Discipling ministry in your church.

"There Is Help for Your Church"

This message communicates the biblical concepts and principles on which we at Churches Alive have built our ministry. These concepts are producing dramatic results as they are applied in hundreds of churches throughout America and overseas.

As president of Churches Alive, Howard Ball spends much of his time sharing these crucial insights to discipleship success across the United States.

— Learn how to begin with what you have and multiply your ministry.
— Learn to avoid common ministry pitfalls.
— Learn how to spiritually motivate your people.
— Learn about a discipling approach that requires a two-year long, weekly commitment from participants — but finds more people wanting to make the commitment than most churches can initially accommodate.

You can be more effective in ministry. *"There Is Help for Your Church"* will help you gain the understanding to make a successful start.

Available on tape cassette or in condensed booklet.
C-60 cassette, $4.50
3⅝x8½'', 30 pages
Illustrated booklet, $.95

Please use Order Form on page 112 or write or call:
Churches Alive, Box 3800, San Bernardino, CA 92413   (714) 886-5361

Growing by Discipling How-to's

For the Leaders ...

A sampling of three guides necessary to conduct the Growing by Discipling plan.

Begin with the *Growing by Discipling Pastor's Handbook,* the administrative guide. Learn how to plan, begin, expand and multiply your discipling ministry so you will effectively serve participants.

Next, study the *Growth Group Leader's Guide,* the handbook to lead the heart of the discipling ministry. Learn how to lead a Growth Group and direct Growth Group leaders in a concept that involves members in a long-term discipleship experience.

Finally, read the *Discovery Class Leader's Guide,* the orientation to new believer training. Learn how to minister most effectively to those just beginning in their faith in Christ. See how to use this approach to introduce other members of your congregation to the benefits of a discipleship group.

Receive all three of these guides and evaluate how the Growing by Discipling plan will benefit your church. These three illustrated 8½x11" books contain more than 300 pages of leadership helps.

Special Leader's Package price, $22.00. You save $3.00 over the single item purchase price.

The Love One Another Bible Study

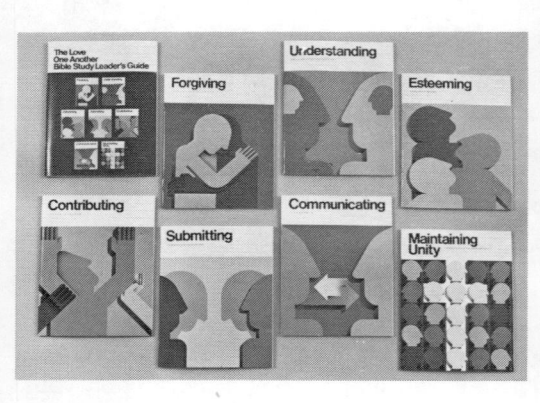

Forgiving
Not allowing anything to hinder a relationship.

Understanding
Approaching things from another's point of view.

Esteeming
Holding others in high regard.

Submitting
Allowing God to lead me through others.

Contributing
Helping others fufill their potential.

Communicating
Conveying truth with love.

Maintaining Unity
Upholding the oneness God gives me with others.

The Love One Another Bible Study Leader's Guide
Complete lesson plans for every chapter in every book.

You will be guided through the essentials of developing close personal relationships — relationships that strengthen your marriage, your family and your church.

Love One Another is endorsed by pastors and laypeople throughout the country because it is Christ-centered, biblically sound and fun. You will enjoy the application exercises that bring your study beyond just theory into active living. The 7x9" books are creatively designed with attractive graphics, many group discussion questions and concise chapter summaries.

And you can use *Love One Another* in a variety of ways. It was written as a course of study for Growth Groups. Many churches are also using this unique course for Sunday School classes and mid-week Bible study groups. Pastors find the lessons useful in counseling sessions to guide people through the complexities of interpersonal relationships.

The *Love One Another Leader's Guide* will equip you to lead people through the series in either a discussion group or classroom/lecture setting.

Individual books, 7x9", 60 pages, $2.00
Set of seven books, $12.00
Leader's Guide, 7x9", 86 pages, $3.00
Set of seven books and Leader's Guide, $15.00

Design for Discipleship Bible Study

You can learn more about the wealth that is available to you in Jesus Christ through this exciting Bible study series. On your own or in a group you can discover what it means to be a Christ-centered disciple, how to develop Christian character, how to have victory over sin and how to grow toward maturity in your daily walk with God.

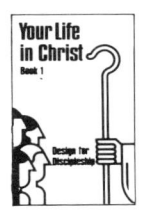

Book 1 — Your Life in Christ

Book 2 — The Spirit-filled Christian

Book 3 — Walking with Christ

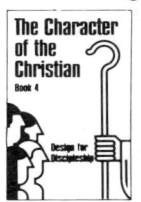

Book 4 — The Character of the Christian

Book 5 — Foundations for Faith

Book 6 — Growing in Discipleship

Complete set (Churches Alive's special 6-book edition), $8.00
Individual books, 5½x8½'', $1.50

Please use Order Form on page 112 or write or call:
Churches Alive, Box 3800, San Bernardino, CA 92413   (714) 886-5361

God's Family Bible Study

A unique Bible study enabling you to explore with others what it means to be a part of the Church, God's family. In addition to personal and small group study, use *God's Family* as a Sunday School elective or as a project for the entire church — with the pastor giving a series of messages coupled with a homework assignment in the book for the congregation.

A *Leader's Guide Edition* of the study includes the student workbook and special leader's helps for teaching and leading a discussion on each chapter.

Individual copies, 5¼x8¼", 112 pages, $2.95
Leader's Guide Edition, 5¼x8¼", 136 pages, $4.50
God's Family Package: Buy 10 copies and get the Leader's Guide Edition free. $29.50

Learning to Solo Bible Study

Learning to Solo

Lead Growth Group members through the principles of effective Bible study to challenge and equip them to pursue their personal study of God's Word. (*Learning to Solo* is Churches Alive's one-volume edition of Books 7-9 of the Navigators' *Studies in Christian Living.*)
5½x8½", 100 pages, $3.75

Helping People to Solo

Equip Growth Group members to solo in Bible study. *Helping People to Solo* is the leader's guide for *Learning to Solo*. Many lesson suggestions, helps, questions, discussion starters, aids to learning.
5½x8½", 71 pages, $3.00

Disciplining Helps

Helps for Reaching Out

CARING is a simple program designed for your church to help you to match people's needs with volunteer "ministers" who can help to meet those needs.

The CARING package includes three identical guidebooks, one for the coordinator, one for the CARING secretary and one for the person who telephones volunteers. You also receive the CARING training and demonstration cassette.

Special CARING package price, $13.00. You save $3.35.
Additional CARING guides, 58 pages, 5½x8¼", $3.95 each.
Additional CARING C-60 training cassettes, $4.50 each.

Coffee Talk gives you insights into the personal experiences of Barbara Ball. Barbara has been using evangelistic entertaining for many years, both for her women friends and as a couples outreach with her husband, Howard, president of Churches Alive.

Using humor as well as sobering illustrations, Barbara reveals how to prepare, hostess and speak at friendly evangelistic outreaches. You will be entertained and challenged as you read and consider how you can use this ministry to reach out to neighbors with the love of Christ. **5½x8½", 80 pages, $4.25**

Bonus! Hear Barbara Ball present guidelines for holding an informal coffee outreach in your home. Then, listen in as she shares her testimony and the gospel of Christ in a coffee outreach meeting. **C-90 cassette, $4.50**

Special Combination Offer! Order the *Coffee Talk* book and cassette together for $7.75. You save $1.00.

Strengthen Group Discussion

Going Up!
Leadership concepts for small group leaders. Includes how to motivate your group, involve them in discussions, encourage participation, vary the format and more. A great help to creativity as a group leader.
5¼x8¼", 82 pages, illustrated, $3.95

Please use Order Form on page 112 or write or call:
Churches Alive, Box 3800, San Bernardino, CA 92413   (714) 886-5361

ORDER FORM

PLEASE PRINT

Date _____

Name _____

Address _____

_____

Phone (____)_____

Are these materials being ordered for your church?   ☐ Yes   ☐ No
If yes, please complete the following:

   Your position in church _____

   Church name _____

   Church address _____

   _____

   Church phone (____)_____

Pastor's name _____

Denomination _____

SHIP TO — ☐ Me ☐ My church   BILL TO — ☐ Me ☐ My church

How Many?	Description	Price Each	Total Price

Merchandise Total	-	Volume Discount
Up to 40.00	-	*
40.01-70.00	-	5%
70.01-100.00	-	10%
$100.00 & up	-	15%

OFFICE USE ONLY

Order Rec'd _____   Invoice No. _____

Invoice Date _____   Shipping Date _____

Shipped via:
Book post ☐   UPS ☐   AIR ☐   UPS air ☐

Check box to receive Tape Catalog ☐	FREE	FREE
Merchandise total		
Less discount (see chart)		
Sub-total		
Calif. residents add 6%		
TOTAL		

Payment Information:
1. *All orders of $20.00 or less must be pre-paid.
2. Make checks payable to Churches Alive.
3. Mark foreign checks: "**PAY IN U.S. DOLLARS.**"

Prices subject to change without notice.

Churches Alive Box 3800 San Bernardino CA 92413
Phone (714) 886-5361

God's Family Leader's Guide

This section is for both LEADERS and TEACHERS of *God's Family*.

If you are leading a Growth Group or Discovery Class* studying God's Family, you will be working with a small group who are committed to regular attendance and having their lessons prepared. Therefore, you don't have to lecture. You can lead your group in meaningful discussion of the material. This is the most effective way to guide your people to understand and apply these concepts. Their learning is strengthened as they verbalize their answers and participate in the discussion. Also, they learn from each other.

If you are teaching in a classroom setting, such as a Sunday School, you will not necessarily have the same group every week; and some may not have their lessons prepared. You will need to do some lecturing. But, even as a teacher, avoid the "I talk — you listen" routine. Involve the class by having them contribute ideas. Use skits, role-playing, demonstrations, illustrations and other devices to help people understand the concepts.

This Leader's Guide has good ideas, but it is not exhaustive. You should invent additional ideas to help communicate the concepts of *God's Family* to your people. At the same time, depending on your teaching situation, you may not either want to or have the time to use all of the suggestions included here. The important thing is to just use what is necessary to stimulate the members to discuss and participate so that they will receive the maximum benefit from the study.

For more information about Growth Groups and Discovery Classes, you can order our Leader's Guides for those groups. See page 107.

You're in the Family
CHAPTER ONE

Read the parable to the class and discuss it, using some of the questions below:

Think about It

What is the main point of the story?

How has God designed you to fit into His building?

Have you ever felt you were on the trash heap like Curved Brick? When?

Why do you think the builder didn't use Curved Brick at first?

What does this illustrate in life?

Cover the questions in the study booklet. Use some of the ideas below to supplement your discussion.

God's Child

ONE. If you are a parent or a grandparent, excitedly whip out your latest photo of one of your offspring and pass it around to the class, all the time extolling the virtues of this child. Then say, "Do you know that's how God feels about you? He's proud to call you His child and loves to 'show you off' to others. Why is it reasonable to expect God to act like that toward you?"

TWO. What are some names people call others that are titles of honor? How do these titles compare with the title, "Son of God"?

THREE. What are some things we inherit from God?

Born into the Family

FOUR. You can illustrate the need to be born into God's family by the fact that the only way a person can be a physical part of your family is by being born into it. If another person looked like you look, acted like you act, worked where you work and did everything else the same way you do, he would not necessarily be a member of your family. Even if he decided to change his name so he was called by the same name, he still would not be a physical part of your family. The only way to become a physical part of a family is to be born into it. So it is with God's family.

Father of the Family

FIVE. What do you think motivated God to do these things for us? What do you think our response should be?

SIX. Develop a short drama from the story of the prodigal son. You will need actors to play the parts of the two sons, the father and two or three friends of the young son. Present the drama in four short acts. At the beginning of each act, set the scene for the audience. The scenes should be:

1) The young son talking to the father about wanting his inheritance immediately and the father giving it to him.

2) A bar, with the young son sitting with several friends, everyone drinking, having a great time. The son buying drinks and paying the tab.

3) The young son out of money, working as a janitor in a restaurant. The only pay he receives is food left on the tables from the patrons. He talks to himself, saying that he should go on home; and he finally decides to do it.

4) The return back home, his father gratefully receiving him and the older son complaining about the party that he throws.

If possible, use people who can add humor and fully develop each character to act out the drama.

At the end of the drama, ask the class the questions listed in the booklet.

Family Bond CHAPTER TWO

Read the parable to the class and discuss it, using some of the questions below:

Think about It

In what sense do we die if we are cut off from the "tree" of our fellowship?

What are other ways we, as Christians, are like plants or parts of plants?

What are some things Lila Leaf does for the leaves that are on the far side of the tree? How is this similar to things that happen in God's family?

Cover the questions in the study booklet. Use some of the ideas below to supplement your discussion.

Love Is the Bond

ONE. Draw the chart outline on the chalkboard, completing each square as the answers are given.

Verse 2 indicates two ways we show love for God's family. Are they the same, or can one be done without the other? How does loving God and carrying out His commands show love for His family?

TWO. Have as many people as possible name the demonstration of love they appreciate the most. This will enable everyone in the class to get to know one another a little better.

THREE. Tell a joke to illustrate that we can stimulate people to laughter. Then ask the class to think of ways to stimulate people to love.

The Nature of Love

FOUR. Ask for a poem or paragraph to be read on each of the four topics. After each one is read, ask the group what they could do to develop that quality of love.

FIVE. In the passage studied, the lack of love is associated with the works of the flesh, while love is presented as a fruit of the Spirit. Illustrate the conflict between the flesh and the Spirit with this story:

A man said, "I have two dogs inside me, a white dog and a gray dog. The white dog wants to do good; the gray dog wants to do evil. And the two dogs are always fighting with one another."

When asked which one of the two dogs wins, he replied, "The dog I feed, of course."

What "feeds" the fruit of the Spirit in your life? What "feeds" the works of the flesh in your life?

SIX. Can you think of a person who seems to "exude" love? *How* is that love shown?

Effects of Love

SEVEN. On the chalkboard, list people's answers to both questions. After completing the list, add a heading which says, "Our class — when we love one another" across the top. Ask, "What would help our group be more securely bound together in love?"

EIGHT. Point out that the story of Gloria and Susan is an illustration of effects Jesus said would happen in John 13:34,35.

Ask how people outside God's family become aware of the love between family members.

Family Power CHAPTER THREE

Read the parable to the class and discuss it, using some of the questions below:

Think about It

What does the story illustrate?

How are we like Little Lamp?

What would be a parallel in your experience to Little Lamp trying harder? to being filled with oil?

What could cause you to run out of oil?

Cover the questions in the study booklet. Use some of the ideas below to supplement your discussion.

God's Presence

ONE. Point out to the class that the paragraph just before question one shows that God the Father, God the Son and God the Holy Spirit indwell the believer.

Draw two columns on the chalkboard, and label them "Present" and "Future." Have people give their responses to the second part of question one and list them in the corresponding column.

TWO. Philippians 2:13 says God is working in us to give desire and action. Put the left side of the chart below on the chalkboard. Write the column headings "Desire" and "Action." Then have the class fill in the words "Yes" and "No" to correctly identify each kind of person so that your completed chart is like the one below.

	Desire (Will)	Action (Work)
Growing Christian	yes	yes
Weak Christian	yes	no
Hypocrite	no	yes
Spiritually Dead	no	no

God's Power

THREE. On the chalkboard, list expressions for walking in the Spirit and for walking in the flesh in two columns. Why do the Spirit and the flesh war against one another? Have you had the discouraging experience of making a New Year's resolution and then breaking it before January 7? Would these verses be an answer to why that happened?

FOUR. Ask the class for examples of God's power being shown through weakness in their own lives.

FIVE. After working through the diagram with the class, ask them for examples of presenting your "members" to God.

SIX. Many decisions about physical "life or death" situations are made each day. This passage speaks of a different "life or death." Verse 10 says, "though the body is dead because of sin, yet the spirit is alive because of righteousness." What kind of "aliveness" do you now experience that you did not experience before you became a child of God?

Family Relations

CHAPTER FOUR

Read the parable to the class and discuss it, using some of the questions below:

Think about It

How are you like Cinders?

Cinders left the fire because he was lured by curiosity. What are other things that lure people away from fellowship and may cause them to cool off spiritually?

Do you think the fire should have tried to stop Cinders from leaving? Explain.

Cover the questions in the study booklet. Use some of the ideas below to supplement your discussion.

Brotherly Love

ONE. We want children and young people to have good feelings about their church that will go with them throughout their lives. How can you help provide those kinds of memories for them?

TWO. As the class answers what they think caused the problem, don't try to arrive at one conclusion; but expect a variety of answers.

Building Relationships

THREE. Ask for volunteers to share an experience when they reacted with one of the negative emotions listed in Ephesians 4:31 and to tell what they would have done if they had been tenderhearted instead.

Bring a bar of soap to class to illustrate forgiveness. The soap is used every time there is dirt, to restore a clean condition. Forgiveness is needed every time there is "dirt" in a relationship, to restore love and unity.

FOUR. Put two columns on the chalkboard — one entitled "Acceptance" and one entitled "Non-acceptance." Then have the group list what results from each. This exercise will demonstrate the need for acceptance in God's family.

Ask if anyone is aware of persons, either a single or a couple, who come to your church alone, sit alone and leave without visiting with anyone else. Then ask why they think that happens and what they as members of God's family can do to help eliminate that problem.

FIVE. Draw the chart shown below on the chalkboard. Point out that in a situation where someone is wrong, neither statement is good. Ask the class how they would speak the truth with love.

	Truth without love	What the other person wants you to say	Truth with love
Statement	*I think you are wrong.*	*I think you are right.*	

Church Families

SIX. Ask the group if they can think of a home where great love and respect is shown between the family members. Then have them describe *how* that love and respect is demonstrated. Point out that this is the kind of love and respect which also should be demonstrated in God's family.

SEVEN. Spend the last three to five minutes of the class time having everyone encourage one another. One way to do this is by smiling, shaking hands and saying, "I'm glad you're here." Tell everyone to be as creative as possible.

Family Needs CHAPTER FIVE

Read the parable to the class and discuss it, using some of the questions below:

Think about It

How does the story illustrate meeting needs in God's family?

Who does Bright Sun represent?

What are some ways Earth Planet's "creatures" helping each other are *not* like God's family helping each other?

In what sense is Earth complete in itself? In what sense is it not complete? In what sense is God's family complete in itself? In what sense is it not complete?

Cover the questions in the study booklet. Use some of the ideas below to supplement your discussion.

Material Needs

ONE. The story of the Church continues beyond what is written in the Book of Acts and could contain a chapter on your church. Discuss with the class things that could be put into the chapter about the family members in your church caring for one another.

TWO. Ask for volunteers from the group to tell about when they were in need and were given material aid by others. Ask them to tell about other benefits from the experience. Encourage them to be alert to people to whom the Lord might have them give assistance.

THREE. If you were not sure whether a person had a legitimate need, what would you do?

Inner Needs

FOUR. Illustrate the principles of Philippians 4 on the chalkboard, using the diagram on the next page.

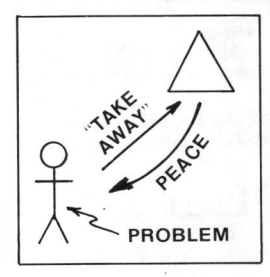

The first illustration pictures a problem that causes someone to experience frustration, depression or some other need.

The second illustration shows a person asking God to remove the problem.

The third illustration shows God giving peace to the person who prayed, even though He didn't remove the problem. Peace that comes from the removal of a problem is understandable. But peace that comes even though the problem is still there is beyond human understanding; it's a special gift from God.

FIVE. Ask the group if any have experienced problems like Paul's and if those problems resulted in an inner need. Discuss whether it is more important to minister to the problem or to the inner need created by it.

Communicating Needs

SIX. Is it wrong to feel any of these needs?

SEVEN. Put two columns on the chalkboard, one headed, "Why needs are not communicated," and the other headed, "Why help is not given." Fill in the columns with the class members' responses.

Family Worship — CHAPTER SIX

Read the parable to the class and discuss it, using some of the questions below:

Think about It

What three things caused Young Pine to want to worship God? What causes you to want to worship God?

Young Pine worshipped God by lifting his arms to Him. What are things that you do to worship God?

Cover the questions in the study booklet. Use some of the ideas below to supplement your discussion.

God's Worthiness

ONE. When you meet together with God's family for worship, what specifically can you do to focus more on the worthiness of Christ?

TWO. If someone asked you why you worship God, what would you say?

Your Worship

THREE. What is the difference between worshipping in spirit and in truth, and what would be the results of one without the other?

FOUR. Ask the group which attitude or action is most important to them and why. Then have them close their eyes while you read Psalm 27 slowly and reverently. Ask them to share what they felt while you were reading.

FIVE. Review the first chapter of Job for a similar experience of worship in the midst of trial. What do the experiences of David and Job tell you about why, when and where you should worship God?

Worshipping Together

SIX. Ask the group to share experiences of how God ministered to them in a particular way as they were worshipping Him.

SEVEN. Have several people in the class give their ideas on the first part of this question. As they do, write them on a piece of paper to give to your pastor or other church leaders.

Conclude your meeting by spending a few minutes in worship. You may want to begin by reviewing what you have found regarding who God is and what He has done (see question 2). You could use several of the ways of worship which came out of your discussion of question 7.

Family House — CHAPTER SEVEN

Read the parable to the class and discuss it, using some of the questions below:

Think about It

What do the flowers represent?

What is a spiritual parallel to owning a greenhouse? to being a garden?

What is the difference between the flowers and plants in the greenhouse and a garden? How does that illustrate a church?

What are some good reasons for wanting to own a "greenhouse"? What are some good reasons for not wanting to own one?

Cover the questions in the study booklet. Use some of the ideas below to supplement your discussion.

Do not spend too much time on questions one through three. They are meant to give the students an appreciation of what it means to be a temple of God as brought out in question four.

The Tabernacle

ONE. Ask the group to imagine being one of the Israelites observing the tabernacle, the cloud and the fire, as related in Exodus 40:33-38. Then ask them to tell how they think that experience would have affected their attitudes toward God.

The Old Temple

TWO. What does it mean to be holy?

THREE. When Jesus said the temple was "your house," the Jews understood that He meant it was no longer God's house.

Read Matthew 27:50,51 to the group. The events described here reinforce the fact that the temple was empty. The veil was torn from *top* to bottom, indicating that God did it. It is also an indication that He left the Holy of Holies.

When the Jews went into the temple and saw the veil torn open, they could see inside the Holy of Holies. Before this time, this would have meant death because they would have been desecrating God's sacred place. But since God had departed, it was no longer sacred. It was just another room.

The New Temple

FOUR. How does (or should!) "you are not your own" affect your daily life?

What are some ways we can "glorify God in our bodies"?

FIVE. As the people give answers for the implications column of the chart, help them develop their thoughts to the point where they see applications for their lives.

Buildings

SIX. Have you ever gathered for worship in your home with other Christians? with your family? Were there differences from worshipping at your church building? Explain.

SEVEN. People may have various answers, but be sure to cover these essential points:

God's Temple Today	Church Buildings
People are God's temple.	Buildings are where God's temples meet.
People are most important.	Helpful but not necessary.
We need to keep our temples holy and treat others with respect.	

Family Conflict CHAPTER EIGHT

Read the parable to the class and discuss it, using some of the questions below:

Think about It

Does anyone here know why rams butt heads?
How is that like what people do?

The other animals were disturbed by the butting. How do you react when you are near tension between two people?

What do you think are the main reasons tension can exist between people in God's family?

Cover the questions in the study booklet. Use some of the ideas below to supplement your discussion.

Disunity

ONE. These passages refer to unity as agreeing on earth, being gathered together in Christ's name and/or being one. What do you think it means to "be one"?

TWO. Develop a short skit, with three or four people arguing about which denomination is the greatest. Afterwards, read the passage and ask how it applies to the people in the skit.

Curing Disunity

THREE. As you cover this question and reference, be sure the group is aware that the rest of the chapter talks about forgiveness. With this concept in mind, help them see that we should approach others about their offenses only when we can do it with an attitude of forgiveness.

FOUR. If you can, bring a small item needing restoration to class. Use it as an object lesson. Otherwise, ask the questions, "What is involved in restoring an antique piece of furniture? How is that like restoring a brother?"

FIVE. Do you think these solutions would seem practical to people who are not a part of God's family? Explain.

Handling Tension

SIX. Put two columns on the chalkboard, one headed "Action" and the other headed "Attitudes." Ask the group to look up the reference and to call out ideas they get from it to be listed under each of these two columns.

SEVEN. Ask for examples of essentials and non-essentials.

Family Goal CHAPTER NINE

Read the parable to the class and discuss it, using some of the questions below:

Think about It

What are lemmings and what do they do?

How are people sometimes like lemmings?

If any of you have ever had the experience of trying to get answers to life's questions when no one seemed to understand you, would you please describe it?

What should you do if you feel you are just running and not accomplishing anything?

Cover the questions in the study booklet. Use some of the ideas below to supplement your discussion.

The Commission

ONE. What motivates you to want to help fulfill the Great Commission? What are the greatest obstacles to being involved? How can you overcome them?

TWO. What happens in your spiritual life if you only take in? What happens if you only give out?

Jesus' Disciples

THREE. Ask the group for ways in which outreach is like fishing.

FOUR. If you were really convinced that your evangelistic efforts were going to be successful, would you do things differently?

FIVE. What are some ways you can take up your cross today? (Galatians 2:20 may give you some additional ideas to discuss.)

Being a Disciple

SIX. As each specific action is listed, discuss how to develop that action.

SEVEN. How have other churches and individuals contributed to your growth as a disciple?

Family Team <small>CHAPTER TEN</small>

Read the parable to the class and discuss it, using some of the questions below:

Think about It

In what ways is God's family like an army of ants?
In what ways is God's family different from an army of ants?

If you have ever had feelings like Anthony, would you please describe them?

Can you give an illustration of how teamwork has accomplished "the impossible"?

Cover the questions in the study booklet. Use some of the ideas below to supplement your discussion.

Teamwork

ONE. After discussing why an army needs teamwork, ask, "What can happen when one unit of an army fails to perform its function?" After discussing why a body needs teamwork, ask, "How does a body respond when one part malfunctions?"

TWO. What makes a Christmas or birthday gift especially valuable to you? Does this say anything to you about the gifts the Spirit gives to Christians?

THREE. Share examples of situations where there have been obvious demonstrations of a variety of gifts but the same Spirit.

Team Goal

FOUR. Draw the diagram on the chalkboard. Ask the group to give reasons why gifts may not be focused on the family goal.

FIVE. What are some ways different gifts contribute to the goal of making disciples?

Team Members

SIX. Ask a volunteer to give an example of how someone in God's family really cared for him/her.

SEVEN. Have two volunteers stand in front of the class. The first volunteer should say, "I can't do as much as others, so I guess I'm not of much use." Then ask the group to find the statement that corresponds to him in 1 Corinthians 12:15-21 and to show him that he is wrong. Have them continue the argument back and forth until they explore some of the implications of the scriptural statements. The other person should say, "I don't need others; I can do it myself." The group should find the statement in 1 Corinthians 12:15-21 that corresponds to him, and then tell him that he is wrong. Again, have them continue the argument until they explore the implications.

Family Leaders — CHAPTER ELEVEN

Read the parable to the class and discuss it, using some of the questions below:

Think about It

What are ways people are like Waylon?

What kinds of decisions do people like to make for themselves?

What are advantages that you enjoy from having leaders?

Cover the questions in the study booklet. Use some of the ideas below to supplement your discussion.

Requirements for Leaders

ONE. Draw the chart on the chalkboard. As you list the ideas from the group, draw conclusions for these three areas.

Can a person truly succeed in one or two of these areas but fail in the other one or two? Explain.

TWO. Review the different ways in which your church family and your natural family are similar to one another. This will help everyone see why a leader in the church needs to be a good leader at home.

Instructions for Leaders

THREE. You may want to consider a class project to help your pastor fulfill his responsibilities.

FOUR. It is the wolf's coming that reveals that the hireling does not really care for the sheep. What exposes hirelings today?

FIVE. What are some characteristics of sheep?

    Why do sheep need a leader?

    In what ways are we like sheep?

    In what ways are we not like sheep?

Results of Good Leading

SIX. Make a paper chain like the one pictured in the diagram, large enough to be complete with the answers. After discussing the links, cut them with scissors to illustrate that if one of the links is broken, the following links will fall.

SEVEN. What do you think leaders should do to help you do the work of the ministry? Be careful that people don't have a critical spirit if their leaders are not helping them as much as they should.

Family Commitment CHAPTER TWELVE

Read the parable to the class and discuss it, using some of the questions below:

Think about It

Why do you think Horace decided not to try to be a bee?

What commitments would Horace have had to make to become a bee?

How is a beehive like God's family?

Cover the questions in the study booklet. Use some of the ideas below to supplement your discussion.

Commitment to God

ONE. Ask for specific explanations of what it means, in practical terms, to present one's body as a living sacrifice.

———

Ask volunteers to share experiences that resulted from obediently following through on a commitment to God.

TWO. After discussing the two questions in the book, ask, "What do we gain when we make this kind of commitment to God?"

THREE. Draw the diagram below on the chalkboard, and say, "This diagram will help summarize some of the thoughts from this question. Your commitment to a leader results in obedience. A leader's commitment to you results in caring."

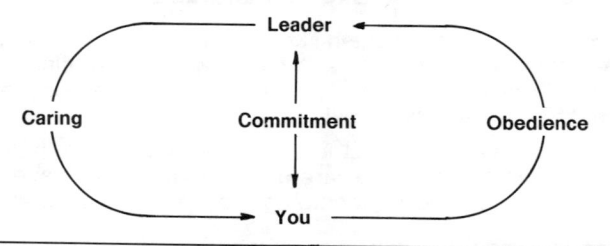

Commitment to the Family

FOUR. Have people tell personal examples of commitment in action.

FIVE. Take a few minutes to quietly consider the examples given, and make a commitment to God of one thing you will do to demonstrate love.

Evaluating Your Commitment

SIX. Bring several paper cups to class, along with two dollars in pennies. Label the cups with typical places people put their treasure (fun, home, business, savings, food, clothing, church, etc.). Place some coins in each of the cups in random order. Explain that the money represents someone's entire treasure and the cups are where this hypothetical person has placed his treasure. Ask someone to come to the front, look in the cups and determine where this person's heart is. Then get another volunteer to come up and rearrange the money so that it would be in keeping with God's desire for his life.

SEVEN. Rather than discuss the answers, have a time of prayer in which people can express their thanksgiving and commitment to God for being a part of God's family.